The E-WORD

ALSO BY CATE MONTANA

Unearthing Venus: My Search for the Woman Within
The Heart of the Matter: A Simple Guide to Discovering Gifts in
Strange Wrapping Paper (cowritten with Dr. Darren Weissman)
GhettoPhysics: Redefining the Game (cowritten with Will Arntz)

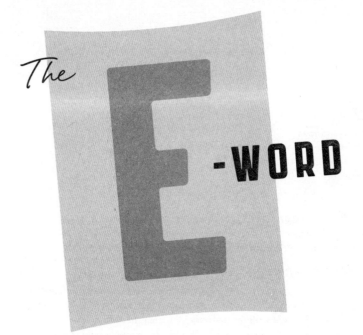

The

E-WORD

EGO, ENLIGHTENMENT & OTHER ESSENTIALS

CATE MONTANA, MA

ATRIA

—

ENLIVEN BOOKS

New York London Toronto Sydney New Delhi

ATRIA BOOKS   ENLIVEN

An Imprint of Simon & Schuster, Inc.
1230 Avenue of the Americas
New York, NY 10020

First Enliven Books hardcover edition January 2017

ATRIA BOOKS / ENLIVEN and colophons are trademarks of
Simon & Schuster, Inc.

For information about special discounts for bulk purchases, please contact Simon &
Schuster Special Sales at 1-866-506-1949 or business@simonandschuster.com.

The Simon & Schuster Speakers Bureau can bring authors to your live event.
For more information or to book an event, contact the Simon & Schuster Speakers
Bureau at 1-866-248-3049 or visit our website at www.simonspeakers.com.

Interior design by Renato Stanisic

Manufactured in the United States of America

10 9 8 7 6 5 4 3 2 1

Library of Congress Cataloging-in-Publication Data is available.

ISBN 978-1-5011-2353-5
ISBN 978-1-5011-2354-2 (ebook)

*For Rhiannon and Robert and all the other women and men
in this world who needlessly suffer because
they don't know who
they really
are.*

CONTENTS

———

The E-WORD

INTRODUCTION

——

After much dithering, I finally decided to introduce this book to readers the same way I introduced it to a publishing friend in New York when he asked me about its early stages in an email:

Your book on ego sounds daunting. How are you approaching it? You love taking on big projects, don't you?! ☺

To which I replied:

The E word? Daunting is right. But for none of the normal reasons. It's daunting because it's so damn simple. And trying to explain simple to humans is so damn complicated.

I'm coming at it from the only place I can come at it from anymore—from Truth. And Truth is really *really* simple . . .

I am

That's it.

I AM is not a story. It is Truth. But just one word tacked onto I AM turns it into a story and thus an untruth.

I am . . .

just is.

I am human . . .

is a story.

I am Cate Montana . . .

is a story within a story.

I am the human Cate Montana and a writer . . .

is a story within a story within a story.

A tale within a tale within a tale

obscuring Truth.

How did I come to Truth amid all these stories and tales? Well, that's a story in itself. But since humans are stories and stories are what we understand best, I figured perhaps there's value in the telling of it. So . . . that's how I'm approaching the topic of the ego. Stories and Truth balancing and (hopefully) explaining one another.

To which he wrote back:

Oh, Cate! I LOVE it! Wonderful!!!

Wonderful? *Yay!*

Cate Montana, writer, was thrilled at the encouraging words. (Writers take every scrap of reassurance they can get.) But he hadn't been kidding when he used the word "daunting" to describe writing about the ego. How do you write about an invisible veil of perception that arrives with birth, coloring everything? About an imperceptible matrix of thought concealing the glorious Truth of who and what humans really are?

Holy crap.

How do you reveal the womb to the child gestating within?

———

DECADES OF HARD INNER work and some twenty thousand hours of meditation had bludgeoned me into a state of clear vision about the ego and how it operates. But, I swore to myself I'd keep quiet about what I knew because I thought there were already enough teachers talking about spirituality and the ego. The world didn't need me wading into the fray.

And then my friend Rhiannon died.

I sat at the foot of her bed, listening to her sister crooning soothing words as she tenderly stroked her hair—the last chemotherapy-surviving wisps of red from her once-thick mane—and something inside me cracked.

Death's presence doesn't suffer foolishness.

The measure of Rhiannon's remaining breaths on this Earth could be counted in a handful of minutes. As I sat in the darkened bedroom with her family and dearest friends, my mind flashed to the many puzzled conversations that had taken place among those closest to her during those final weeks.

Rhiannon was dying of brain and bone cancer at age fifty-three. What had brought her, of all people, to this end? She was beautiful, successful, and brilliantly talented. She had many friends and a loving partner. On the spiritual path for decades, she seemed to have everything going for her on every level.

But she couldn't see it.

She put on a good face, but underneath she was profoundly unhappy, deeply stressed, and angry.

People wondered, "Why was she this way?"

Why had she felt so unfulfilled? So lost? What had tormented her so?

I listened, over and over, to the same questions voiced in hushed tones over tea, coffee, and wine in Rhiannon's living room as she lay semiconscious in her bedroom down the hall . . . all the while knowing that I actually knew the answer.

And so as my friend drew her last shallow breath that cold March night, even as tears of sorrow and relief began to flow, I resolved to be silent no longer.

PART 1

A Little Background . . . Story

1

QUESTIONS

How can we be here and not wonder at the miracle of existence?

It all started when my dog ran away.

Actually, it started a lot earlier than that.

Like most kids, I asked a ton of questions growing up. "Why is the sky blue? Why do I have to go to school? Why can't I eat ice cream for dinner?" And answers to questions like that were reliably forthcoming.

But answers to the really interesting questions like, "Who am I? Why am I here? What is life? What is God? What is death?" went unanswered. I was told there were no answers to such questions, so it was best not to ask.

Which shut me up temporarily.

But the questions never went away. As I went about living a "normal" life I just lost track of them for a while.

I went to school, got a degree, developed a great career in the (at that time) exclusively male bastion of network sports television, got a dog, made money, got married, bought a house with a swimming pool, and then got divorced and sold the house with the swimming pool.

It was the move from the big house with the big yard in suburbia that did it. What large, self-respecting, half collie, half German shepherd would tolerate a small midtown Atlanta apartment? Apparently not my dog, Merlin. After screaming myself hoarse and plastering his picture on every telephone pole in a two-mile downtown radius, in desperation I finally took a friend's advice and went to see a psychic.

A rather plump, matronly woman named Virginia assured me Merlin was okay. "He's all part of the plan, dear," she said soothingly. "Don't worry. He'll be back in"—she closed her eyes briefly—"eleven more days. Now . . . let's talk about you."

What about me?

I didn't care.

But she wouldn't back off. As often as I tried to lead the conversation back to my dog, she kept bringing it back to me. Apparently I was not doing what I'd come to planet Earth to do. I was fiddling while Rome burned. I needed to clean up my act. I needed to quit smoking and get a handle on the booze. I needed to exercise. I needed to move back to the country (I'd been raised on a farm). I needed to get in touch with my Higher Self.

I needed to meditate.

Really?

I paid and left feeling unsettled. I was relieved to hear Merlin would come back. Not that I totally believed it. But the rest? What a load of hooey. And then, after lots more driving around town calling his name, crying, and poster plastering, exactly eleven days later, Merlin came home.

Hmm . . . how the hell did she know?

THAT SIMPLE QUESTION OPENED the floodgates. If she'd been right about my dog, what about the rest of what she'd said? It wasn't like I was actually happy or anything. Network sports television, while exciting and lucrative, was also stressful and exhausting. I hated living in the city. And drinking and smoking, both of which I did a lot, made me feel like crap.

Why not make a change?

Within a month I'd found a great condo on the Chattahoochee River next door to a state park north of the city. I bought a kayak and started paddling the river. I hiked with Merlin. I danced. I quit smoking and dropped the hard liquor, diving into an exploration of fine wines instead.

And I started meditating.

Why not?

All I had to do was close my eyes, put my hands in a funny position, and look within. I mean, how hard could it be?

Right.

OKAY. I GOT IT. A crazy person was at the helm.

A crazy person with a mind that contradicted itself and never shut up and yet had nothing interesting to say. A crazy person who was restless and couldn't sit still, who felt anxious and nervous over nothing, whose brain couldn't hold a coherent thought for more than fifteen seconds.

And why bother trying? My most profound thoughts revolved around sex, food, money, and the latest sitcom plot. What was there to hold on to?

So much for self-discovery.

But I persevered. After all, there had to be *something* in there . . .

And so every night I sat up in bed and looked within for hours (if I could stay awake) watching the *yadda yadda* in my brain that was, apparently, the sum total of "me."

Talk about depressing. But then, after about six months, something extraordinary happened.

I'd drifted off to sleep sitting bolt upright (as usual), when suddenly, I was aware of a bright light and high ringing tone all around me. The light got brighter until it was LIGHT. The ringing got louder. The most awesome ocean of LOVE swept through me. I became aware that the light was actually a being.

I woke up, scrabbling around in my blankets trying to get on my knees to bow down to this being. And yet the light still filled my mind and I could still feel the love and hear the ringing. So I cried out to the being, "Who are you?"

And the most enormous, gentle tide of laughter rolled through me—laughter that was infinitely loving and very familiar. "You'll know someday," came the answer. Not in words. And yet the understanding was crystal clear in my mind.

Then gradually the light and the ringing presence and the love died away. And I was left, once again, with questions.

2

THE JOKE

—

With Truth comes the "peace that passes all understanding," because with Truth there is no need for understanding. All beliefs, ideas, and insights are equally illusory stories.

What's to understand?

Understanding there is no understanding—understanding that the attempt to understand is the very thing that obscures Truth—isn't a philosophy. It isn't an "understanding." And it's not a concept you can grasp.

It's the end of grasping . . .

After my encounter with the light and what at first I imagined had been God himself talking to me, I began my spiritual journey with a hell of a lot of grasping.

I wanted answers . . . fiercely, obsessively. And year after year I sought them.

Bypassing the Episcopal and Catholic religions of my youth—whose priests had been the ones telling me that answers about life and the divine were unknowable—I dove into the astonishing world of New Age spirituality.

Ascended masters, angel guides, alchemical tales of immortality, new revelations into the Apocalypse, ancient traditions such as Taoist philosophy and exotic Eastern teachings into chakra systems and kundalini energies, out-of-body experiences, tarot, Wicca, and meditation—it was like being catapulted into the Technicolor land of Oz after growing up in black-and-white Kansas.

Surrounding myself with others of like spiritual mind, I read the same books everybody did, learned the same techniques, arrived in the camps of the same gurus, went to the same seminars, and paid to hear a lot of people spout variations on the theme of "enlightenment"—which was, apparently, what I was looking for.

The ultimate place of ultimate answers.

The Holy Grail of Holy Grails, the password to infinite bliss and all-knowing knowingness . . . people who were really spiritual sought enlightenment. So I sought enlightenment too.

Proudly I set foot upon "The Path." And soon I was surrounded, not with hard-drinking, foul-mouthed TV production guys, but soft-spoken Birkenstock-wearing New Agers sharing thoughts about the latest books they'd read, the name of their guru, and the best organic rice cakes to buy at the co-op.

It seemed all answers lay before me—answers about death, life, the source of my unhappiness, the truth about the light that had greeted me—if only I could read enough, meditate enough, be good enough and pure enough and disciplined enough to find them.

I'd been a high achiever ever since I woke up my freshman year in high school and, despite my boredom with the subjects being taught, decided to study and do well. My ego just couldn't handle continuing the role of classroom dunce. Now I transferred all the fervor and energy I'd once spent on my studies and on developing my career and my love life into my search for enlightenment.

And because I was a nice spiritual person, I wanted everybody else to get enlightened too. Never mind that deep in my heart I hoped I'd get there first (at least before all my friends did). That's just human nature.

Part of the prize is getting there ahead of others.

At least it was for me.

FOLLOWING THE TEACHINGS OF a female Christian mystic, I gave up coffee and other things like meat and television and polyester . . . whatever I was told and (more important) believed was keeping me from "it." She also heavily promoted chastity—so I didn't study with her for very long.

Sex *and* enlightenment. Surely, despite religious dogma to the contrary, it was possible to pursue both?

I pursued.

But somewhere between lovers after my divorce from husband number two, sex began to lose a bit of its luster. Not that I was giving it up or anything. It's just that marital status and sex didn't seem to have quite as much to do with happiness as I'd once thought. With more time available, I plunged more deeply into my quest for enlightenment.

I went back to school, studied the mind, and got a graduate degree in psychology.

I went to a New Age channel who taught some intense breathing techniques.

I read a ton of spiritual books.

But mostly over the years I did my own thing, which was sitting, eyes closed, rigorously looking inward. I called it "meditation," because that's basically what meditation is. And I did it for hours and hours and hours and hours and hours and hours and hours.

I looked within for days and weeks and months of hours.

I arranged my life around my inner pursuit, quitting my TV career and starting work as a freelance journalist writing from home.

My love life went on hold.

And it all paid off.

I had lots of cool psychic experiences—moments of bliss, moments of oceanic Oneness, moments of elevation and revelation, out-of-body experiences, lucid dreams, and visions. I healed a wounded bird with my touch. I levitated (not much, but for a few moments I was floating!).

Thirteen years of cool experiences passed.

Fifteen.

Eighteen.

And then I got it.

And the joke was on me.

––––––––

NOTHING HAS BEEN MORE desperately disappointing—or funny—than lusting after enlightenment for twenty years only to finally realize I could never, ever get it no matter how long or hard I tried, because:

Cate is a story.

And the absence of story is enlightenment.

Thud.

Yeah, the Truth is not hidden. How many times have we read the whole "there is no 'I'" business? It's even a movie. Remember *The Matrix*? The whole point of the film is Neo waking up to the truth that his identity and everything else in the Matrix isn't real.

And how about the little bald kid in the Oracle's living room telling Neo, "Do not try and bend the spoon. That's impossible. Instead, only try to realize the truth . . . there is no spoon. . . . Then you will see that it is not the spoon that bends, it is only yourself."

Wow.

It sounds so profound. And it is, mostly. At least it would have been if the kid had shut up after he said, "there is no spoon." But he didn't go far enough. Because the truth is, not only is there no spoon, there's no "yourself" either.

But after I'm done being all impressed with the Truth that there is no spoon and no "me" either, what am I left with?

Me and a spoon.

Dammit, it's right there in my hand—all solid and woody feeling—the tip chewed up from when I stuck it too far in the blender one morning making some disgusting good-for-me green drink. Which I still drink most mornings because it's good for me—never mind I know there actually is no "me" and no green drink and no freaking spoon.

A woman's got to keep up appearances.

3

THE DREAM OF CATE

—

Personal identity is a terrible burden and the only real cross we bear in this world. To have it lifted is joy beyond human comprehension.

It was somewhere around year twenty on The Path that my personal identity and the illusion of worldly appearances in general began to crack.

The ego "I" naturally started falling away during meditation, making room for what, back then and today, I can only call "nondual awareness"—a blissful state of unity consciousness where the separate sense of self disappears, opening the door to an awareness of the much vaster ocean of consciousness referred to as I AM.

After all those years of hard work, you'd think I would have been thrilled at the accomplishment. You'd think I would have danced with joy, shouting to the heavens, "I finally achieved samadhi (divine consciousness)! Hooray!"

But I didn't.

I couldn't cheer and I couldn't take credit, because the state itself made it quite clear that "I" hadn't achieved anything at all. Samadhi occurred *despite* me. It happened *without* me.

Grace arrived upon my departure.
The absence of me *was* bliss.
How the hell could I own that?

———

PLUS, IT DIDN'T SEEM to have any effect on my life.

After a few hours in meditation not being me, I'd open my eyes, get up, and spend the rest of the day being me—writing articles for newspapers and promotional copy for environmental businesses, engaging a personal life that included a new partner (yes, I resuscitated my love life!), two hybrid wolves, two cats, twenty acres of yard and gardens, lots of friends, and all the typical drama that comes with being a human being . . . with anxiety over money issues topping the list of consistent worries.

Morning nirvana was great. But the nondual state of consciousness didn't persist two milliseconds after I opened my eyes and got off my meditation pillow. Which frustrated me to no end. What good was bliss and unity if they were only available with my eyes closed?

But I persevered. What else was there to do?

Bliss is . . . well, blissful. Yes, part of me wanted to run back into the cave, close my eyes, and make bliss a full-time job. But I had a partner I loved. I had responsibilities. And after twenty years of seeking I wanted *balance*.

Enough with the weird separation between spirituality and normal human existence. Surely there was a way to be in the world and yet not deluded and pained by it? A way of being that was whole and happy . . . even blissful . . . while at the same time productive?

Surely the state of Oneness and unity that arrived with my eyes closed would eventually wear away the "normal" physical sense perceptions of separation that gave me the daily "me" filled with anxiety and fear . . . the isolated ego called "Cate" who lived in a deeply divided and screwed-up world.

I'd gotten this far. I just had to keep going.

――――――

YEARS PASSED.

My journalism career flourished.

I was hired by the filmmakers of the indie hit *What the Bleep Do We Know!?* And suddenly, as editor of the film's monthly newsletter, I found myself interviewing quantum physicists from CERN like John Hagelin, neuroscientists and doctors like Stuart Hameroff, writing articles about everything from superstring theory, quantum foam, and superposition to reviews on the latest consciousness studies.

I was thrilled to be bringing information about mysticism and science to the world in such a major way. Finally, I was combining my work and spiritual life!

And how did all this mesh with my daily excursions into Oneness?

It didn't.

But certain things were becoming clear. For example, I realized the dualistic state of the human ego was a lie of perception that truly created a dream world. But not in the way the majority of spiritual people and texts would have it.

The world itself isn't a "dream" per se.

It's the illusion of separation and duality we experience living in the world that's the dream.

But how to get beyond the illusion?

I was still torn between two different realities: unity and bliss at dawn followed by fourteen hours of separation and not-bliss. In fact, that's what I called them—the two realities. I even started writing a book titled (rather unimaginatively) *The Two Realities*.

I talked with my spiritual friends, assuming they were wrestling with the same issue, but was met with blank stares. Finally it was Rhiannon who tipped me over the edge, making me realize such conversations were futile.

We were at a mutual friend's house for Thanksgiving, sitting in the living room, drinking wine, inhaling the great turkey smells, having a good time, when I casually mentioned "the bliss of the absolute Truth of Oneness in deep meditation."

"How can you know what you experienced is the truth?" Rhiannon said, instantly on the attack.

"Uh . . . because it's not me experiencing it. It just . . . uh . . . is," I replied, not surprised, but a little taken aback by the flames suddenly shooting from her blue eyes.

"That doesn't make any sense," she snapped.

Back in those days making sense was really important to me, so I struggled with words, trying to explain the obvious that I was rapidly grasping wasn't so obvious.

"There is no 'I' knowing anything in those moments," I said, making finger quotes. "Knower and known are the same. There's just seamless is-ness with no separate 'me' around noticing it. And that's, um . . . Oneness . . . the state of Truth."

"But how can you possibly know it's the truth?" She was really pissed now. "How do you know you're not fooling yourself?"

"Because in those moments there is no self to fool, Rhiannon. There is no 'me' around."

"But how do you know you're not fooling yourself?"

I gaped at her, flummoxed.

"How about another glass of wine?" I asked, dropping the subject.

I never talked about Truth again until now, writing this book. Strange that it was Rhiannon who finally reopened the door.

———

AND THEN ONE DAY on a cool September morning I opened my eyes after meditating in the yard and . . .

There was no "I" around.

Well, well, well . . .

I got up and strolled past the gardens toward the bottom gate of the yard. I say "I" because there's no other way of putting it without sounding ridiculous.

What I mean is, there was no personality around to do anything "normal" with the information that was arriving through the eyes, ears, nose, skin, and tongue—no normal "Cate" reactions or thoughts, like feeling dissatisfied with how the flower beds were looking and stopping to pull some weeds.

"I" laughed. There was no one home to judge anything. Which is when it hit me that not only was there still no sense of a personal "I" around, the deeper truth of the matter was:

"I" had never existed in any meaningful way in the first place.

Between one footfall and the next, the entire illusion of "Cate" was revealed.

I looked around and could almost see it—a scintillating holographic network of neurons in the shape of a human brain suspended in midair; a tangle of concepts sparkling insubstantially in the early autumn light; a cobweb of make-believe; an intangible information hub holding my birth, childhood, thousands of boring classroom hours, my marriages, my orgasms, my careers, my hopes and dreams . . . everything.

All the information input of a lifetime dangled in front of me. *And I thought this was me?*

Laughter bubbled up from the gut—a great Buddha guffaw where the joke is cosmic in the extreme and you finally "get it." Except there was no one home to get anything . . . and that was the joke.

Cate Montana didn't exist.

She never had—at least not in any real way. She was a fabrication; a mental construct created from physical experiences and perceptions starting at conception that created neuron patterns that, firing in the brain in the right order, continuously produced the identity that labeled itself "Cate."

More laughter. So that was how identity was built! Layer upon layer, data bit by data bit—like a computer program being constructed—until *voilà*! There was a sense of a distinct, separate self.

The ultimate story.

What a joke! Cate Montana was a *short story of the mind . . .*

I looked downstream along the river of time and saw no death waiting for me, only the flow of eternal life. If my body had dropped dead in that moment it wouldn't have mattered a bit. Nothing would have changed.

I glanced upstream and saw that I had never been born. All there was and ever had been and ever would be was eternal I AM.

Awareness of existence

containing existence.

Simple as that.

MY PARTNER WAS AWAY at a business retreat, and for three days I simply existed. I ate when hungry and slept when tired. I left the phones shut off and ignored the computer. Frankly I don't know what I did those three gorgeous days except simply live. What more needed to happen?

When Tess came home she could tell I was in a completely altered state. Which, of course, wasn't true. Cate was the altered state, not I AM.

"I hope I'm not disturbing you," came her voice from behind the shower curtain the night of the third day.

Disturb? What a concept. "Don't worry," I said, laughing. "There's no one home to disturb. You could drive a brass band through the house. I wouldn't care."

But the next morning the threads of Cate began to re-form. Thoughts began to take on personal significance.

It's Monday.

Instead of a simple observation, the thought suddenly carried personal implications. There was work to do, an interview to prepare for, ads to invoice. It's not that I'd forgotten these things before. It's just that they'd held no relevance. Three days had passed with barely a thought in my head.

But now, like contrails in a spotless blue sky, thoughts with personal meaning attached began to criss and cross, gradually hemming in the infinite, defining something, giving it boundaries and limits.

"Cate" was taking shape once more.

Everywhere I looked there were cobwebs. They wove between stems of grass. They interlaced the slats on the backs of lawn chairs. They shimmered among the topmost branches of fir trees in the yard, glistening deadly traps for the unwary insect.

Delighted at the obvious metaphor, I laughed, thinking *humans are indeed caught in webs of their own mental making. I mustn't let myself be caught back in personal identity again.* Uneasily I noticed I was thinking like Cate again, giving my "self" advice.

Let go, I thought, and immediately felt dismay.

Only a limited, personal self would have anything to let go of.

I spent the afternoon of day four dropping into meditation on and off, trying to prolong the freedom of not being me. But by dinner I'd lost the battle pretending the old neural patterns in my brain weren't firing once again.

For weeks I moved into and out of nondual awareness, struggling against the noose of my personality. Driving the car or sitting in front of the computer, I'd catch myself mentally chanting *let go let go.*

Then I'd remember that having the thought of "letting go" was establishing the reality of a separate self that had something to let go of . . . and identity would blessedly slip away.

4

AFTERWARD

—

You cannot dissolve an illusion by focusing on it.

The slipping in . . .
     and out . . .
     of the dream of Cate . . .
has been going on ever since.

Sometimes it happens for a few minutes. Sometimes it happens for hours or a few days. I've finally realized this in/out process of shifting perception is just how it is. There's absolutely nothing I can do about it one way or the other. I can't make myself lose the perception of my human self. I cannot dissolve an illusion while remaining in its grip.

There's a wonderful example of this truth in Richard Bach's book *Illusions*.[1]

Richard and his spiritual teacher, Donald Shimoda, are lying on the grass in a field, taking a break from flying their biplanes. Richard is practicing mentally dissolving an enormous thundercloud growing on the distant horizon—a task Shimoda has given him.

In his mind he throws heat rays at the cloud. He zaps it with laser blasters. He tries crushing it and dissolving it. The thundercloud keeps growing. Finally Richard gives up in disgust. "No matter what I do, that cloud just keeps getting bigger," he says.

Shimoda glances lazily over his shoulder and says, "What cloud?"

Of course, when Richard looks again, the cloud has disappeared.

———

PERSONAL IDENTITY (THE EGO) is like that cloud.

You can't kill it.

But here's an important news flash: You don't need to.

All you need to do is know that it's an illusion and not what or who you really are and then proceed with life accordingly. Which is easy for me to say now. But back when all this first happened, I didn't have a clue what proceeding accordingly looked like.

Within five months of that glorious and shocking three-day transition into what was (depending upon which Eastern yogi's definition you read) a high state of *nirvikalpa samadhi* (a bliss-filled state wherein all illusions are dissolved), my life in the States—my business, my partnership, my home—fell apart.

How would it not?

It wasn't "my" life in the first place.

For two years I traveled on the money from the sale of my house . . . Peru, Ecuador, Chile, Costa Rica, Panama, India . . . rootless, directionless, rudderless. Everything had been peeled away— passion, career, purpose, partnership, love, friends, home, possessions, pets—even the languages spoken around me were not my own.

Looking back, the reason for all this is clear. The light had dawned. I finally knew I wasn't really "me" at all. And so all the things "I" clung to as part of my identity naturally fell away. And yet, dammit, I was still "me."

A me that was totally lost and confused.

Coming back to America I settled again in the Pacific Northwest and plunged back into writing, gradually coming to terms with what was left on my human life's to-do list.

Number one was: let go of all attachment to liberation.

Equally important was consciously making sense of my experiences (which weren't really "mine" at all!) and assimilating the paradox of being both fish *and* fowl—of being both red *and* blue in the rainbow. I had to understand how I could understand the enlightened mind while being unenlightened—stuck in a state of consciousness that contained both points of view:

Unity

and

Duality

A place I still am.

A state of consciousness I have finally (*yay!*) come to recognize in psychological terms as the *transpersonal mind-set*, a normal state of awareness that all humans will evolve into someday; the *transition state* between personal (ego) consciousness and the transcendent state of egoless enlightenment.

I had learned about this state of consciousness in graduate school and then promptly forgotten about it. My (ego's) obsession with enlightenment—my need to resolve my black-and-white, two-realities conundrum (ego versus no-ego) and get from one state to the other as fast as possible—and mental conditioning to see things in terms of absolutes and either/ors (a highly patriarchal ego trait) were so great I'd completely missed the fact that:

The evolution of human consciousness is a process.

There is such a thing as gray in our world.

There is an in-between stage of ego expansion (not ego inflation) where we are set free to be our divinely human selves—a consciousness that can be developed that is literally capable of creating heaven on Earth.

The existence of this state of mind and the pathway to it weren't clear to me for ages—certainly not in time to do my friend Rhiannon any good. But it's clear now. And that's what this book is about: helping people wake up to the limited nature of the ego and vault into a whole new level of awareness and functioning called *transpersonal consciousness*, where the ego identity is expanded to include humankind, cosmic experiences, and life in general.

It's also about clearing up people's confusion about enlightenment.

Enlightenment is not an expansion of identity. It's the annihilation of identity. "Divine suicide" is how a teacher once aptly put it. Which is *not* what the vast majority of seekers are looking for.

People want happiness and fulfillment, creativity and compassion, community and connection, abundance and love, adventure and ease. And *that's* what transpersonal consciousness delivers. It's the fabulous middle ground where you still are "you" and yet you are unhooked from the tyranny of the ego, liberated from the suffering that arises from the ego's illusion of separation, aware of being united with the greater whole, fully conscious that personal identity is just a convenience and the natural by-product of living in a body.

Sounds great, doesn't it?

People say enlightenment is the ultimate liberation. But transpersonal awareness is also liberation . . . the kind of liberation you can enjoy because you're still around to enjoy it. The other great thing about transpersonal consciousness is that, unlike spiritual enlightenment, transpersonal consciousness can be directly cultivated.

Which is no small blessing—a blessing that comes, quite frankly, in the nick of time.

During the late stages of assimilating all this, I became hyperaware of not only how dysfunctional the ego is, but how catastrophically dysfunctional the world the ego has created really is.

In spiritual circles, materialism rages and the Law of Attraction absorbs everyone's attention. The ability to manifest vacations and shiny new cars is now a hallmark of spiritual superiority. In some circles it's a competition. Enlightenment—the ultimate deconstruction game—has been turned into an acquisitions practice.

In the mainstream, fundamentalism—Islamic, Judaic, and Christian—is making a global comeback and Christian fundamentalism is making strong gains in American politics.

Hard-won women's rights are slipping away.

Corporate greed and political corruption continue to escalate out of control.

Terrorism is pressing people to choose between security and freedom.

The climate is changing faster than the news can report. Oceans are dying while the fight over fossil fuel exploitation escalates.

Almost everybody is reduced to the impossible task of trying to turn dollars into happiness—and failing.

And all of it is happening—*all of it*—because the nature of human perception, the role of the ego, and the matrix of illusion it spins have *never* been explained in a fashion that makes these things socially relevant enough for people to want to address the situation and change.

And yet for the very first time in human history, we have

the education and tools to put our global ego insanity under the microscope and transcend it. There are ways to talk about the perceptual prison we're unknowingly trapped in. Concepts and scientific evidence that have never existed before can now be used for a wholesale broadening of human self-understanding—ideas that can elevate and unite us while avoiding the emotional mine-fields of religion and spirituality.

The term "matrix" is a prime example.

Today it's a common word that most people understand means an environment or pattern in which something develops and is held. So when I talk about the "ego matrix," we already have the sense of it. Even better, because of the film *The Matrix*, a lot of Westerners subconsciously get that I'm also talking about an invisible program that molds life as we know it, giving us an utterly fabricated, false reality that is taking us to our doom.

Pretty good for one word.

———

YES, THE WORLD IS dealing with a deadly ego matrix. And it's time for us to swallow the red pill and catch on before it's too late. And spiritual/religious people, sorry: Almost all spiritual and religious people have *two* red pills to get down because they're dealing with a double whammy: a regular ego matrix *plus* a spiritual/religious ego matrix.

Yikes!

But hey, it's just where we're at in the evolution of human consciousness—an inevitable and uncomfortable stage of growth we all have to get through, like junior high school. But here's the deal:

To get through it we first have to know about it.

We can't change something we're unaware of. And becoming aware of the ego's nature while still being stuck in the ego's matrix is the tough part. Once we see it, once we know what's really going on and where we're at and why all the crap that's happening in the world is happening, *then* we can actually change.

Not before.

So . . . onward and onward.

I'D LIKE TO ADD one last thought before we dive into an exploration of the ego and its web of illusion. When I first got into spirituality, I thought the following line from the the Bible contained great wisdom:

> *Seek ye first the kingdom of God . . . and all these things*
> *shall be added unto you.*
>
> —MATTHEW 6:33

But to glean the wisdom I had to realize the kingdom of God referred to isn't some fantasyland in the sky.

Cooperation, harmony, abundance, the peace that passes all understanding, ease and grace—the kingdom of God—come from a state of mind . . . a way of *perceiving* self and the world that cannot be realized until the occluding lens of the personal ego is stripped away or at least understood for what it is and put in its place.

Growing up to step into our natural inheritance where all things are indeed added unto us is not about opinions and arguments, theology and rules and regulations, and attaining and gaining—it's a matter of developing clear vision and individually taking the passionate journey to discover the truth that:

The kingdom of heaven lies within.

It means wiping the sleep from our eyes so we can finally see with the eyes that belong to that kingdom and make it manifest.

So, shall we start the journey and lift the ego's veil? Throughout the rest of the book there are practices at the end of each chapter to help you do just that. One day, if you take the journey, you'll discover there is no veil at all.

PRACTICE: DEVELOPING DESIRE

If you put this book down now and never read another line of this or anybody else's work and simply look within your own being—and I mean *look* and deeply *contemplate* what you find inside—and *ask* for the consciousness of I AM to be made known to you for a sincere and passionate hour a day for the rest of your life, without a doubt your life will change for the better, because this is what I AM responds to and how it is revealed.

Your life might not be *easier*.

But it will be far richer and more fulfilling.

This is how I know to see beyond the ego, enter transpersonal awareness, and begin the kind of change we all want to have happen in our lives. And the method is simple:

1) Consciously desire knowledge of the *real*.

Remember, I AM *is* you and *is* me. I AM doesn't need to be pleaded with or sought or prayed to. I AM doesn't need us to tell it what we want because it *is* us. However, to make I AM known we have to genuinely want to know who we really are.

But in the physical realm, intent and desire are not enough. To call forth the physical experiences that will teach us, mind, spirit, and body must align. Which means action has to be taken. And the aligned action is:

2) Sit and look within and ask, "Who am I?"

And if you say you don't have an hour a day to dedicate to this, then sit and look within for half an hour—or fifteen minutes. But *start*! Do something to get the gears in motion. Be genuine. If you really want Truth, you will be willing to spend the time. If you're not willing to spend the time—and time is our greatest gift on this planet—be honest with yourself. If this is just an intellectual journey for you, read and move on. No worries. The seed will have been planted.

If you want to take action but somehow just can't seem to (and you're sitting around feeling vaguely guilty about it), then the first step is to develop greater passion for self-knowledge. Or maybe looking within scares you. *What will I find?* But even so, you think it sounds important. In both cases I suggest you:

Desire the desire for a greater consciousness.

Let the desire for Truth beyond all opinions and theologies and philosophizing of egos be your deepest, most passionate goal—the thing your heart and soul and mind hunger for most.

And if you're wondering "How do I develop greater desire for Truth if I lack sufficient motivation to take the time to focus on finding Truth?" all I can say is this:

Desire cannot be forced. Action can.

Hold a ham sandwich in front of an anorexic and command, "Hey, you! Develop a desire to eat this!" and they'll tell you where to stick the sandwich. Only if they've gotten as far as realizing they're sick and need the sandwich, *even though they don't want it*, is there a chance for change.

The desire to get better will lead them to force themselves to take a bite.

It's the exact same situation with Truth.

Lack of Truth—not knowing who we are—is the foundation of *all* human suffering. If you've suffered and finally reached the point where you're sick of it, even if you don't want to, *force* yourself to sit down for fifteen minutes a day and ask the "Who am I?" question. And if you miss a day here or there, big deal. Don't let your ego use that as an excuse to quit.

Acknowledging your painful human condition by taking action to alleviate the cause of the pain by looking within and asking this will kindle greater desire to take more action.

Action creates more action.

If you know that taking that first bite of the ham sandwich is vital but you just can't do it, ask for the desire to do so.

I know I just said prayer and pleading to I AM is unnecessary because you already are I AM. But there has to be action accompanying intent. Prayer—when there is no other kind of engagement or dedication—is an action. Getting down on your knees and humbly asking for the desire for Truth to well up within you is an action.

It might look like a baby step, but it's not. Any and all steps in the right direction are equal steps in the right direction.

Unlike the ego, the Truth that you are does not judge or measure.

PART II

The Ego Matrix

5

NO JOY IN MUDVILLE

—

There's life and then there are belief systems about it. And never the twain shall meet.

My second husband said that when he was a little boy he thought there was something "off" about the world. "There was just something about it," Simon said. "Life felt fake . . . like a stage play or a TV show to me."

For years he tried to catch the world in the act of lying to him.

If it were raining outside the back windows of his house, he'd race to the front windows to check if it was raining in the front yard as well. Walking down the street he'd whip around as fast as he could to see if everything behind him was still there, hoping to catch ghostly stagehands working furiously on a half-built facade, trying to find faults with the fabric of reality he intuitively sensed were there.

He is not alone in this. Many of us sense the world is not the place it seems to be.

The theme of hidden truths, wheels within wheels, and subterranean realities populates countless books and movies. One of the most famous is the 1999 movie *The Matrix*. Morpheus, one of the main characters, describes it this way:

> What you know you can't explain. But you feel it. You've felt it your entire life—that there's something wrong with the world. You don't know what it is. But it's there, like a splinter in your mind . . .[1]

Formless disquiet: inner puzzlement edging toward fear as the craziness of the outside world increases.

And the craziness of the outside world *is* increasing.

I'm not talking about the natural world. Left alone, life is exquisitely balanced and evidences extraordinary beauty and harmony. Contemplating the interconnecting patterns of energy unfolding as countless spiraling galaxies, trees and forests, ecosystems and animals—the magnitude and unfathomable intelligence of Creation take our breath away.

But instead of reveling in life's magnificence, we trash it.

We slaughter wild creatures into extinction for pleasure and torture domestic animals for profit in industrial wastelands called "farms" that have not a blade of grass or a ray of sunshine within their walls.

We abuse others.

We abuse ourselves.

We weep with loneliness in the night and walk the streets in fear, looking over our shoulders. We serve money and power as indentured servants and groan under the weight of the yoke. Then we raise our children to be the same and take our places.

And we explain this how?

We make up stories.

It must be God's will that all this is so. What other possible explanation could there be? It's human nature. We were made this way as part of some incomprehensible plan.

We pass the buck.

Which enables us to go our merry way, participating in a story where 111 million Americans consume 8 million pounds of guacamole and 15 million pizzas during the Super Bowl, while 25,000 people worldwide, mostly children, die that same day of hunger.[2]

But hey, as long as it's God's plan for us, it must all be okay. Right?

No wonder 26 percent of Americans suffer from a diagnosable mental disorder.[3] Madness is the only possible result of following such a plan . . . global dysfunction the only possible outcome of accepting the absurd, stress-filled lifestyles grinding us down . . . down . . . down . . . blindly riding the wave of our own faulty perceptions into the abyss.

———

IT'S HARD HEARING ABOUT such things and thinking about such things.

Sometimes the only way to bear it is to shrug and say, "That's life."

But it's not life.

It's a *story* we're unconsciously living.

A belief system about "how life is" that has nothing whatsoever to do with how *life* really is and everything to do with how the human ego thinks and operates in a thought matrix of its own making—an antilife matrix that's not a dream, but a nightmare.

Yes, the matrix is real.

It may not be as the Wachowskis depict in *The Matrix*, but it imprisons us just the same. And it's everywhere.

It is all around us, even now, in this very room. You can see it when you look out your window. Or when you turn on your television. You can feel it when you go to work. When you go to church. When you pay your taxes. It is the world that has been pulled over your eyes, to blind you from the truth.[4]

What world? What truth?

Simply put, we live in the world the ego has created.

And the truth?

The ego is rooted in separation, fear, and isolation, a perspective that is, as we will shortly see, quite delusional. But delusion or not, the ego's mind-set colors and informs everything: our thoughts and emotions, our creative endeavors, our relationships, our goals, our beliefs, our hopes and fears and dreams, our cultures, politics, educational systems, and religions.

The ego is all about survival and beating out the competition, whether it's for food and shelter, money, jobs, a beautiful mate, a place in heaven, or simply a good parking spot. It has to have stuff and be the best to compensate for its insecurity. And it doesn't care what it has to do to accomplish this.

This is reflected in our world, where millions glut themselves with guacamole while children starve, where government officials take massive bribes to vote against environmental legislation that will ensure the future health and well-being of their own grandchildren.

We live in an ego matrix—a web of thoughts and beliefs that becomes our identity determining who and what we think we are and what we're capable of becoming—a crushingly narrow viewpoint that programs our every action and choice.

An anorexic young woman, her ego programmed by distorted

media-based body images, looks in the mirror and sees a fat person. She hears the voice in her head screaming, "You're fat! You're a pig! You're disgusting!" And she chooses not to eat.

Programmed by fear, entire nations close their borders and minds to others in need, install massive security protocols, and restrict personal liberties in exchange for perceived safety.

Several studies indicate that as few as 13 percent and possibly as many as 56 percent of ten- to fourteen-year-old Western girls engage in various forms of self-mutilation on a regular basis.[5] Like zoo animals trapped in a cage with no way out, many young girls cut themselves with razors in bathrooms and dreary hideaways to try to dull their emotional pain, their souls crying out for spaciousness and beauty . . . for something real and valuable to nourish their minds and hearts.

But all they have is the matrix:

A perception-based, self-reinforcing ego story . . .

a living feedback loop that defines our lives.

An invisible prison we cannot smell
or taste or touch.

A prison for our minds
that arises from our bodily perceptions
obscuring the Truth
of who we are
and the real and beautiful nature
of existence.

WELL, CRAP. HOW DO WE GET OUT OF AN INVISIBLE PRISON?

THAT IS THE SIXTY-FOUR-THOUSAND-DOLLAR question.

The great teachers like Buddha and Jesus have been trying to wake us up to the illusion of the personal self and the matrix the ego spins for millennia. They're the ones who first explained what's going on by saying such things as:

"I am awake" (Buddha).

"My Father and I are One" (Jesus).

These two statements couldn't be more different. Yet both accurately describe the perceptual state available *outside* the ego matrix. Unfortunately, to fully understand what is really meant by both statements (and pretty much everything else Jesus and Buddha ever said), we have to be outside the matrix like them as well.

Which we aren't. Which means as nice as their words are we're pretty much stuffed.

What to do?

Well, first we have to get our heads into a different game. And to do that we have to realize there *is* another game.

Simple peasants thousands of years ago were too ignorant to understand things like perception, psychology and consciousness, quantum physics, and evolution. The information didn't even exist. As a result they had to be given childish allegories pointing toward the truth because that's what their minds could deal with.

But we're not children anymore.

Quantum physicists using rigorous scientific methodology to plumb the farthest regions of reality, probing the foundations of Creation itself, have discovered that beneath the mask of physicality, the whole of life is actually a *nonphysical unified field of energy and information.*

In the social sciences, transpersonal and evolutionary psychologists like Abraham Maslow and philosophers like Ken Wilber who have studied human consciousness have figured out that life is like a series of nested Russian dolls—you know, the tiny painted figures that are placed in identical but larger structures that get progressively bigger and bigger?

That's how we are.

Human consciousness starts out very limited in its understanding of how life works. As we get older individually and as a species, we grow in awareness and subtlety of mind until we finally embrace the next larger pattern of life.

Like everything else, human consciousness is evolutionary.

Can we understand, from our current mind-set, what Buddha and Jesus were saying? Not quite. But we have a far better shot at it than our forebears. Individually and collectively we can include more and better data in our "reality" in order to deliberately upgrade ourselves beyond the immature ego stage of life and get to the state of consciousness they taught about.

"In my Father's house are many mansions," says John in the Bible.

Every level of consciousness, every grade, every nested doll, every mansion is its own "matrix."

Every level of consciousness we experience is a web of information and understanding that expands beyond the previous level.

And step by step, room by room, mansion by mansion, we evolve in awareness until one day . . .

All the matrices vanish.

PRACTICE: TUNING INTO THE MATRIX

Watch the film *The Matrix*. Even if you've seen it before, watch it again with an eye toward becoming aware that the world you know is a programmed illusion. Afterward, contemplate:

1) Have you ever had the feeling you're missing something about life? That there's more going on than meets the eye?

2) Does the world and where it's going make sense to you? Or does it feel as if everything is slipping out of control?

3) If our institutions and governments, belief systems and goals are all part of a thought matrix built by the limited personal ego that knows only separation, isolation, competition, survival, and fear, do world conditions start to make a little more sense knowing this?

4) Does it make sense that the human species grows in consciousness just like a child grows to learn and understand more about itself and the world?

5) Notice where public (and private) voices of evolving unification, compassion, and peace are clashing with less mature voices, practices, actions, and beliefs that inspire fear and ever-greater conflict between people(s).

6) Imagine a different way of understanding self and the world that can heal our current ills—a mind-set of unity and brother- and sisterhood that clears away fear and competition, making room for compassion and peace.

GROWING UP

—

*Life never ends
and thus neither does evolution.*

When I was working on my master's degree in psychology, I discovered a system for understanding the evolution of human consciousness called Maslow's hierarchy of needs, developed by Dr. Abraham Maslow, one of the founders of transpersonal psychology and the fourth force of psychology.

The needs hierarchy provides a very clear picture of the process of moving through the various levels of personal ego function until the big breakout into transpersonal awareness finally occurs.

Briefly, Maslow believed that humans evolve through six levels of consciousness. Each level builds upon its predecessors, and a reasonable integration of all the experiences and awareness gathered from the previous levels needs to be acquired before a person moves to the next level of consciousness. Personal evolution past any given level is not guaranteed. And an individual may operate in several different levels simultaneously.

Take a look at the following diagram. The bottom level of consciousness in Maslow's hierarchy is based squarely in what?

MASLOW'S HIERARCHY OF NEEDS

Physical needs.

It's hard to argue that before anything else, a human being requires air, water, food, rest, sleep, and a sexual, procreative outlet. These are basic survival needs, and until they're all satisfied, life is most often a brutal struggle that can entail horrific experiences, decisions, and actions.

As we get farther into the book, you'll understand how grasping the *physical root of the ego* is critical to understanding the immature ego nature, outlook, and goals. For now it's enough to know that our basic psychological existence and mental health requirements start at the physical level.

After fundamental physical issues are handled, our needs increase. Safety concerns arise. Having a mere roof overhead gives way to the desire for secure housing—a protected environment safe from future physical, mental, and emotional harm—as well as a certain level of financial or bartering security to perpetuate these things.

If these two most basic levels of physical need are not taken care of it's difficult or even impossible to move on to greater expression in life. A woman who is starving to death, for example, isn't likely to be concerned with philosophy and higher ideals. A man stealing cars to maintain his crack addiction is not focused on his artistic fulfillment.

If physiological and safety needs are met, the next set of needs to show up is "belonging needs"—the desire to be part of a community and family and to have friends as a means of satisfying the human requirement for love, connection, and nurturing.

Once family and social networks have been created and belonging needs are satisfied, something called "esteem needs" quickly follows on the psychological horizon. Being in a group, whether at work, socially, or in a family, the ego develops the natural desire for recognition and respect. The need for self-esteem and the desire for a personal sense of accomplishment and meaningfulness arise.

The desire for "more"—to have more, be more, and know more—is a beautiful thing and is hardwired into us. Part of the definition of life itself is movement and change.

At the fourth level of consciousness, a growing interest in knowledge and beauty begins to develop, as well as a yearning for the fulfillment of such abstract concepts as freedom, justice, and wisdom. Finally, the desire for a more fulfilling life on one's own terms evolves—a life of personal flowering and expression.

This is the fifth level, called "self-actualization," a point of development where the potential of the personal ego is expressed in the highest possible form. Instead of being driven by survival, needing companionship to feel loved, seeking to look good in the eyes of others or feel good about oneself by conforming to social norms, at this level a person is highly self-sufficient and self-defined.

Here the driving need becomes total self-expression for its own sake.

Creativity is the key word of the fifth level of Maslow's hierarchy—and not just creativity in the traditional sense of being an artist. Self-actualized people create a way of life that reflects their individual essence: mentally, physically, emotionally, and spiritually.

Things called "peak experiences" characterize this level— moments where an individual feels fabulously complete, happy, and fulfilled for no obvious reasons at all. Self-actualized women and men embrace the unknown, accept themselves with all their flaws, are unconventional, and enjoy the journey, not just the destination. They have a decided purpose and are untroubled by trouble. They are grateful and experience deep relationships and tend to be kind to just about everyone.

They are also characterized by humbleness and evidence a high resistance to any sort of cultural programming. Many of the world's greatest thinkers, artists, and leaders, such as Thomas Jefferson, Albert Einstein, Gandhi, and Mother Teresa, fall into the self-actualization category.

SELF-ACTUALIZATION SOUNDS PRETTY GREAT, and it is. And yet the first five levels of the needs hierarchy are all firmly locked into the personal ego perspective of being a separate individual—a consciousness that believes itself to be an individual stand-alone unit.

At the fifth level of self-actualization, you are a very mature, happy, and fulfilled person to be sure. But you're still a stand-alone unit.

Interestingly, Maslow originally ended the needs hierarchy at level five. Even today many psychologists and most laypersons perceive self-actualization as the pinnacle of Maslow's system as well as the highest possible level of human experience and expression.

But later in life, Maslow added a sixth level of human operation, which transcended personal needs and strict ego identification, called the *transpersonal* level.[1]

You almost never see it in diagrams, but at this level of consciousness the personal ego has integrated all the previous levels and expanded self-actualization into an awareness of global and/or universal interconnection and a sense of self that extends *beyond* the personal to include humanity and life itself.

The transpersonal level has tapped into the consciousness:

I am

———

MASLOW'S NEEDS HIERARCHY IS not universally accepted, and there are other evolutionary theories of human consciousness. I mention Maslow and the needs hierarchy because his work dovetails exceedingly well with the insights I have gained about the constraints physiological function and needs place upon the expression and evolution of the ego.

Also, his system shows that not only do human beings operate at many levels of ego consciousness, it shows that our sense of self—and the mind-set and concerns characterizing that sense of self—evolves over time.

No one level is better than the other. Is a senior in high school better than a kid in third grade? Of course not. The student is just in a different phase of life.

It also helps to realize that this evolution is highly dependent upon physical circumstances. And the needs hierarchy makes it clear what those circumstances are.

In some parts of the world, vast populations struggle with physical and safety needs. As a result, violence and uncertainty are the norm. The fear characterizing the mind-set of the majority in these nations will continue until economic and social factors are deliberately changed to support a growth in consciousness.

It's equally easy to see the primary psychological mind-set of people in the United States and the majority of citizens in other first-world nations. We're clearly dug in at level four, individually striving to attain greater self-esteem, personal accomplishment, and the respect and acclaim of others.

It's just where mainstream society is at on the evolutionary scale of consciousness.

But here's a question: How long do you think the Earth and humanity as a whole can sustain the assault of billions of egos striving to prove themselves by playing king of the mountain with natural resources, nuclear devices, and economic brinkmanship?

Will we evolve past the perception of self as an individual stand-alone unit in time?

Will a majority awaken to the fact that there's more to us than meets the eye and more to life than we currently grasp? Will the majority of us desire to move in a more unlimited unifying direction before we blow ourselves up or become corporate slaves to the almighty dollar, too tired and too busy to develop independent will and the urge to become greater?

I sure as hell hope so.

The brilliant thing about the needs hierarchy is that it shows us exactly what needs to be provided in order for the world to evolve. And it's not higher fences and bigger bombs.

Third- and second-world nations need infrastructure.

People everywhere need water, food, shelter, safety, and education.

Citizens of first-world nations need to understand that there's an expiration date on ego insecurity, move beyond the chronic need for material one-upmanship, and start playing the cooperation game.

Everything is in place for us to do this!

We've got enough food and lattes, shopping malls and housing. Our minds are brilliant. Our hearts are great. Our spirits are indomitable. Our fingernails are polished. Our bodies are strong from spin class and weight training.

Most of us have jobs and money.

Child abuse is against the law.

Teachers aren't allowed to throw chalk or hit us anymore.

Technologies are advancing at warp speed. Our scientists have looked back in time to the big bang and the start of this Creation, peering into the foundations of matter, vaulting our knowledge to dizzying heights.

We have the Internet and smartphones.

The sum total of human knowledge is sitting on a device in our pockets.

All we have to do is choose to understand human nature and who we are, grasp what our abilities and shortcomings are—which means getting a handle on the ego—put on our Big Girl and Big Boy pants and use all this to consciously move ourselves beyond the first five levels of the needs hierarchy toward a more transpersonal view and a bounteous, mutually beneficial way of life for all.

PRACTICE: WHERE AM I?

Take part of that hour you're setting aside for contemplation and meditation and consider where "you" fall within the needs hierarchy. Remember, most of us have aspects of the "self" manifesting at multiple levels. For example, you might be lonely and in search of a mate in order to fulfill level-three belonging needs while also dealing with the self-esteem issues of level four.

Also, please remember there is no "better than" in this assessment.

1) Contemplate where the majority of your focus and energies are directed on a daily basis. Are you desperately trying to put food on the table? If you're reading this book, probably not. But perhaps survival fears still drive you?

2) Are you chronically concerned with what others think of you?

3) Are you a heavy competitor?

4) Think about the things, fears, and issues that drive you and relate them to Maslow's needs hierarchy.

5) Think about where the "next!" button lies at each level for you. How much safety is enough safety? How much belonging and love is enough belonging and love? How much stuff do you need, how much acclaim or fame before you can finally feel good about your self?

7

WHERE WE'RE AT

—

We call ourselves human beings.
But for the life of me I can't figure out why.

We've got all the basics handled. No more struggling for survival. Now we spend our time and energies massaging our self-esteem by acquiring nicer houses and gourmet takeout, Jimmy Choo shoes, Audis, and ever-more-massive flat-screen TVs.

If the modern world is any indicator, it takes a *lot* of this kind of stuff (and bigger garages) to satisfy the ego that doesn't know there's anything more. So let's examine level-four consciousness by checking out the daily life of Sally Jane from Tallahassee, Florida—a typical human who's doing pretty well acquiring all the things needed to satiate the ego at this point in the hierarchy.

———

EXCEPT FOR THE HOURS she spends chained to her desk at an accounting firm during the week, Sally is constantly on the move. She races through breakfast, battles traffic, flinches at rising gas prices, gets to work, and then can't wait to leave.

After work she runs to the dry cleaner's, dashes to the grocery store, schedules an appointment with her mechanic while waiting in the checkout line, hurries to pick up the kids from their guitar lesson and ballet class, all the while planning dinner, mentally rehashing the quarterly tax statements sitting on her desk, and wondering if the dog's heartworm medication is working.

After Sally Jane and the kids get home, her husband arrives as well. He turns on the TV and the news screams disaster messages. The kids play video games. After dinner she argues with them about doing their homework, cleans the kitchen, then sits down with her spouse to pay bills and tries to figure out how to squeeze extra funds from their budget for the college fund. She's an accountant. She should be able to find the money somewhere.

But she can't.

A second round of depressing news closes the evening. The battery in her electric toothbrush has died, so she adds it to the shopping list on her phone, sets the alarm, and flops into bed, ready to go the same round the next day.

And the next and the next.

But her mind is still on speed dial.

She lies there, reviewing every detail from work, the last parent-teacher meeting, the diminishing value of their stock portfolio, the fight with her mother over moving into assisted care . . . visiting every worry and fear in an endless loop while her husband snores.

At 3 A.M. she adds "schedule doctor's appointment" to her phone notepad to see if she can get a prescription for a sleep aid.

On her thirty-minute lunch break, a coworker advises getting in some time for herself. An article in a magazine at the doctor's office suggests yoga and meditation, aromatherapy baths, and long walks on the beach for destressing. She tosses the magazine down in disgust. Pilates at the gym has become just one more thing on her to-do list.

Meditation? You've got to be joking.

A stunning sunset flaunts itself across the sky as she races across the grocery store parking lot that evening—an improbable riot of oranges, purples, pale yellow, and tangerine. But she doesn't see it. She's fumbling for her car keys, trying to settle an argument between the kids.

Weekends are no better. That's when she catches up on everything she can't get done during the week. She can drink more on weekends, though, because she can sleep late the next morning.

Damn! she thinks. *Did I buy enough mixer?*

Sunday morning Sally lies awake in the dusky predawn hours staring at the ceiling nursing a headache, examining her life.

I've lost myself, she mourns. *Years ago.*

Sometimes, at moments like this, she wonders if there'd ever been a "her" to lose in the first place: a passionate Sally overflowing with appreciation for sunsets and clean, crisp air breathed deep into her lungs. A Sally who dreamed at night of the grand things she would do and the amazing person she would become. A Sally who woke up every morning with a smile, languorously stretching under the covers like a cat in a warm pool of sunshine, her mind reaching outward, eagerly anticipating the day.

Had a person like that ever existed?

She can't remember.

Such is the tragic life of

the typical modern Western human being

trapped at level four.

*And if there's any being in there aside
from being busy . . .*

I'll eat my hat.

PRACTICE: STOPPING

Remember that hour a day I recommend taking for knocking on
I AM's door? I still recommend it. But for a while I suggest taking
thirty minutes of that hour and instead of more "doing" (even
meditation), I recommend *stopping*.

Dear heaven, give yourself a break.

You don't have to join an ashram or quit your job or leave
your kids and find a cave to *stop*. You don't have to put money
on a charge card. Just find thirty minutes a day. And if that thirty
minutes is divided into two fifteen-minute pauses, fine. This is not
about doing things right. It's about letting all that pressure go.

BUT

That said, remember this: The ego is all about self-importance.
And how self-important is not being able to find thirty minutes a day to commit to working toward the consciousness of
wholeness?

Which "I" is so busy?

If you're a woman, this is especially difficult. We usually come
in last on the to-do list because we're so often focused on other
people and their needs. But this too is an ego trick.

"But my children, my husband, my staff. If I'm not there for
them every second of the day and night, what will happen?"

What will happen is that *you* will change. You'll embody a
different kind of priority for others to witness. And what a gift
that reflection will be for them!

There is no "process" for stopping any more than there is a process for dropping a hot potato. But here are a few pointers:

1) Keep your personal time sacred. Yes, life happens. Don't stress if this time gets cut short occasionally. Roll with it.
2) It doesn't matter where you stop or when. But outdoors is always best. Nature is one of I AM's best ambassadors and doorways.
3) Turn off phones and iPods and music devices. Listen to the silence. Listen to the wind, the birds, your breath, the kids on the distant playground. Listen to life.
4) Do not be dismayed if doing nothing drives you a little crazy at first. Or a lot crazy. Doing nothing is against *every* ego program in the book. Which is one of the reasons it's such an excellent exercise. Fidgeting, watch glancing, foot jiggling, hair twirling, and other general signs of anxiety are normal decompression.
5) Don't try to stop your thoughts. But don't sit there thinking about work or the dog's vet bill or your kid's school bullying problems either. If you're going to think about anything, contemplate how amazing life is. Contemplate what you've learned about the ego and I AM.

Calm down and breathe.

Put the "being" back in being human.

8

AN OVERZEALOUS ASSISTANT

—

*No wonder we ignore global warming and starving children.
Who has the emotional capacity and mental strength to deal with
that at the end of the day?*

Sally Jane wants to care about the world. So does her husband. They have kids. They're good people. But they're both tapped out. So Sally adds "ignoring human suffering, corporate greed, and the destruction of the global ecology" to the stack of other issues in her guilt closet . . . and closes the door.

She hardens her heart and toughens her mind.

She quickly learns to flip past the haunted eyes of children from the Sudan staring at her from the magazine ads, silently pleading for aid. She turns off the news showing thousands of dying sea lion pups washing up on the beach in California.[1] Learns to ignore the emaciated polar bear standing on a five-foot square of ice surrounded by a thousand miles of water.

She learns not to feel.

She learns not to care.

It's the only way she can survive.

EVERYBODY "GETS" THIS PICTURE, because it's a snapshot of the mansion in consciousness the majority of Western humanity currently inhabits. So let's continue learning about the invisible cause behind all this frantic doing and misery.

For starters, I'd like you to imagine something.

Imagine you have a lot going on (no problem), the ambition to make something of yourself, and the money to hire a twenty-four-hour assistant to handle details for you.

This assistant does the paperwork and filing, writes the shopping lists, researches which car to buy, which stocks to invest in, does the taxes, and basically runs your business and organizes your life. Day in, day out, nighttime too, this wonderful person does all the tasks that must get done.

Then one day you realize your assistant is abusing his authority.

He's screening your calls. He only lets certain people get to you. He starts calling the shots on everything . . . from the clothes you wear to the people you date to the kind of house you can buy to the books you read to how you can wear your hair.

He never shuts up.

Worse, he badgers you and constantly puts you down, saying things like, "You're just as stupid as your father always said. No wonder you're not doing better financially."

What would you do with an out-of-control, interfering jerk like that?

Give him the boot, of course!

But guess what? You already have exactly this kind of helper in your life right now. And you can't give him the boot because your full-time assistant is . . .

your mind.

Which shouldn't be a problem, because the mind, along with our opposable thumbs, is one of our greatest tools and gifts. But this particular gift has been turned into an affliction because our assistant has been possessed, hijacked by a delusional control freak called the ego.

Instead of "me" using my mind as a tool to run my life, my ego is in charge and I don't even know it!

Why?

Because

I think the ego is me.

Even though it's just thoughts and opinions in my head—a verbal processing stream as my brain recalls, associates, and organizes information—over time this flow of consciousness, reflecting an erroneous point of view created purely from sensory impressions experienced through my body, becomes my personality—my *person*-ality.

But my personality is not "me."

The personality is a mental construct that ends up with a name attached to it like Cate or Sally or Harry or Joe. And over time this idea of "self"—this ego consciousness—becomes so potent (in the mind) that by sheer inference and association it unconsciously gains a Facebook page, cell phone number, and Social Security card.

Cultural belief in the ego's reality as "me" and "you" has gained such acceptance that the Merriam-Webster online dictionary defines ego as "the self, especially as contrasted with another self or the world."[2]

But how did this weirdness—this case of mistaken identity—happen?

Believe it or not, it started with a mistranslation.

Ego in Latin means "I am." It is the first-person conjugate of the verb "to be."

The nineteenth-century creator of the psychoanalytic method Dr. Sigmund Freud is credited with using the word "ego," along with two other psychological terms, the id and the superego, to describe specific mental structures in the human psyche. Which brings us to another dictionary definition of ego:

> One of the three divisions of the psyche in psychoanalytic theory that serves as the organized conscious mediator between the person and reality especially by functioning both in the perception of and adaptation to reality.[3]

But here's the rub. Freud never actually used the word "ego." That was a mistranslation of his words from German to English by James Beaumont Strachey, a nineteenth-century British psychoanalyst and translator of Sigmund Freud's work. The terms Freud actually used were *das Ich*, or "the I," *das Es*, or "the It," and *das Über-Ich*, or "Super-I," which Strachey interpreted as the ego, id, and superego.

Nor did Freud view the ego as the "organized conscious mediator between the person and reality." Freud originally proposed that the role of *das Ich* was as moderator between the instinct-based id (our animal urges) and the autocratic inner voice of fatherlike discipline and authority, which he called the superego.

It sounds complicated, but once we get past the academic language, the concept is simple: Freud labeled the different voices jabbering in our heads every moment of every day the I (ego), the it (id), and the superego.

Here's a quick example of these voices in action:

A married guy is walking down the street on a warm spring day. A young woman in a short skirt and blouse with a plunging neckline walks past. As his head automatically swivels to get an ass shot he thinks, *God, I'd like to get some of that.*

This is the instinctual voice of the id.

That's the problem with you, boy, snarls a second inner voice. *You're always thinking with your goddamn gonads.* This is the voice of the authoritarian superego.

A third voice chimes in: *Dude. Sure, she's pretty. But you love your wife and know better than to go there.* This is the moderating voice of the ego.

We all have various forms of these kinds of internal conversations. But because of a mistranslation, the rapid popularization of psychology in the twentieth century, and a wholesale Western obsession with the mind, everyone now uses the word "ego" when referring to the vocal collective providing an endless, conflicted mental running dialogue—basically a whole lot of shit in my head that I can't shut up—as "self."

And yet all we're really talking about is a stream of words through the mind.

What a shock it was when I finally understood that all the blah-blah and images, memories, opinions, fears, and worries comprising my inner dialogue weren't me!

I was sitting on my meditation pillow one morning with all this garbage floating through my head when all of a sudden I thought: *Wait a minute! Is this what is meant by my ego? Is this my personality . . . my image? Is this what's keeping me stuck?*

It was like Neo from *The Matrix* waking up and seeing the Matrix for the first time.

The voice in my head had so totally been "me" that even with all the books and retreats and ahas, I'd never gotten that *this* was what I was supposed to be dealing with, not getting my palm read another time or buying another book.

This is what my husband, Simon, had been looking for all those years ago as a kid. The lie drawing a curtain across the real world: the matrix of the ego mind and all the words in the brain covering up the calm, spacious Truth underneath:

I am.

By the end of this book I passionately hope that you will have seen it too.

PRACTICE: WHO AM I?
This is an enormously revealing thing to do.

Sit where you won't be disturbed. Turn off the phone. Take a moment to relax. Now ask yourself this question: Who am I?

Say it aloud or think it:

Who am I?

Answer the question.
Take as long as you want.
Write down your answers.

———

I DON'T KNOW ABOUT you, but my ego only has one answer to the "who" question and it's "Cate Montana." Like that really says anything!

But seriously, what other answers did you come up with besides your name?

And if you've written down things like, "I'm a man" or "a woman" or "I'm Hispanic" or "Caucasian" or "a college graduate" or "a mechanic" or "I'm nice" or "I'm happy," then stop. These are "what" answers.

Not "who" answers.

I was shocked the first time I did this exercise and it continues to confound me that, besides my name, I can't come up with a single other "who" answer. And of course, since I'm not really my name, this leaves a gaping blank that can only be filled by:

I am

HONEST SELF-REFLECTION IS VITAL for getting a handle on the ego mind. And it's tough, because at the beginning of the process the ego *is* the self. What's to reflect on?

"I'm just being me. What are you talking about? What do you mean I'm not being my real self? Of course I am!"

So observe the stream of words in your brain. Become what Eckhart Tolle, author of *The Power of Now*, calls "the watcher."

As you drive to work, leave the radio or your headphones off. Don't listen to music or the news. Listen to *yourself*. Pay attention. Grab whatever moments you can to do this—in the shower, jogging, grocery shopping—or how about skipping the eleven o'clock news? What a trade! Instead of soaking up thirty minutes of murder and mayhem right before you go to sleep, use the time to get cozy in bed and sit gently with yourself.

Start tuning inward. And if you have a partner/lover/husband/ wife, invite them to join you.

Try not to react to what you observe going on in your head. Don't judge what you think about. It's *all* okay. Don't try to change your thoughts. You don't have to do anything. Just watch.

That's it. That's the start.

9

WHO?

––––

Make friends with silence.
It's the best relationship you'll ever have.

So what lies behind all the blather in our brains?

What supports it?

When I make a statement like, "I should have been working on my taxes, but my thoughts strayed to the cat," who is the "me" behind the word "my"? Who do "my" thoughts belong to?

When I say something like, "My ego is out of control," what am I really saying? Who owns the ego that's out of control?

Please think about this for a moment.

If we want out of the ego matrix, we have to understand who the real owner of our mind and body and ego is. Getting to the transpersonal level in consciousness—the state of mind in which we move beyond purely personal concerns into a greater awareness of our interconnection with others and life itself—means we need to become aware of the "I" that isn't the ego mind all wrapped up in thoughts about better orgasms, making money, and wanting to become more spiritual.

We need to become aware that *somebody else is home.*

We need to discover the silent, watchful "presence" beneath the rat's nest of body-mind-ego thoughts and emotions—a voiceless presence unconcerned with opinions and knowledge, untouched by emotions, and unharmed by body aches and pains—a presence with no identity whatsoever.

Consciousness itself.

Which is what

I am.

SO WHAT IS CONSCIOUSNESS?

Merriam-Webster defines consciousness as "the condition of being conscious: the normal state of being awake and able to understand what is happening around you."

The ego is a conscious point of view that gives us one specific perspective, an ability "to understand what is happening around" us that is *always* highly self-centered and grounded in our physical experience and knowledge base.

For example, a guy you don't know gets inside your personal space at a party and you feel uncomfortable. Your "understanding of what is happening around you" is that he's coming on to you and you don't like it. So even though he's really interesting you rebuff him.

But he isn't coming on to you. He was raised in India, where personal space boundaries are much more intimate than in the United States. But the "you" you think you are can only interpret the encounter in one way because of how body-mind-ego "you" has been programmed by past experiences.

The brain stores the information of every thought and smell, fright and moment of pleasure. Everything we ever experience is carried forward in our subconscious mind. And every thought we have and every action we take reflects these past experiences. It's impossible for us to encounter another human being (or anything else) without dragging a load of background programming in the form of thoughts, judgments, and opinions along for the ride.

The programming of the past is inescapable.

Let's say you're overweight and on vacation and want to join some people on a walking tour. The guide says, "This is a difficult climb requiring a certain level of fitness."

If you're even slightly overweight it's highly likely you're sensitive about it. And being sensitive it seems to you her gaze flicks over your flabby waistline as she says this. You immediately feel hurt, bow out of the walk, and spend the day nursing resentment in a coffee shop eating chocolate croissants.

The woman means nothing by the comment. And she really didn't check out your waist. But this is what the ego does with moments like this. It takes what is simply a fact—it's a difficult climb requiring a certain level of fitness—and twists it into a personal insult because that's what the ego does: It takes everything personally *because that's all it knows.*

It's built from your personal past . . . quite literally from your *person.*

Instead of hearing the woman and thinking, *Hm. It's a steep climb. I'm not sure I'm up to it. Maybe I'll go to a bookstore instead,* her comment gets filtered through your ego matrix and all its crap about weight and every picture of every model you've ever seen in *Cosmopolitan, GQ,* or on Instagram, and your desire to look like them and all your self-hatred because you don't, and the time in eighth grade when none of the boys would dance with you, and how your stepfather called you "big butt," and . . . blah-blah-blah.

We only see what our upbringing, experiences, education, training, knowledge, and bodies will let us see. We are programmed to hear only what the personal filter of our ego will let us hear. We are possessed by a matrix of perception that won't admit any other view, because dammit, it's *my* view.

Mine!

This is the prison we dwell in.

BUT WHAT LIES BEHIND our ego's programmed thoughts and issues? A silent witnessing presence that is pure consciousness.

There is no "my" in pure consciousness. Just awareness.

No commentary. No opinions. No right or wrong.

Just awareness.

Many people have names for this invisible, reclusive "I"—commonly known as the witnessing presence—residing behind our programming. Eckhart Tolle in his book *The Power of Now* refers to it as the "silent watcher" behind the mind.

Helen Palmer, enneagram expert and author of several books about this system of personality typing and self-observation, calls the witness aspect of us the "inner observer."

The Buddha himself advised the practice of mindfulness and becoming self-aware—not just of the myriad voices in our heads and our emotions, phobias, compulsions, and habits that comprise our personality, but of the presence that lies *behind* all that ego stuff, giving it life.

Taoism is all about uncovering "the way," which is the flow of the One, the foundation of life found in each one of us.

Psychologist Arthur J. Deikman, author of *The Observing Self*, talks about discovering and using the "observing self," as well as the difference between modern psychology and the mystical traditions in terms of consciousness. Modern psychology, he says, focuses on our thoughts, emotions, and issues—the *contents* of consciousness. Whereas the mystical traditions of Buddhism, for example, focus on becoming aware of the pure state of consciousness—pure awareness—upon which the contents of consciousness are built.

And while it might seem like a difficult task getting in touch with this inner presence, nothing could be further from the truth.

It is simplicity itself.

Unfortunately, the ego loves to complicate things with a lot of fuss and muss, because complexity is one of the ways it wields control and gets to feel important. One major way I complicated my search for pure awareness was through a whole lot of personal study. I think I must have believed I could *read* my way to I AM! And one of the first things I read about was Buddhism.

The Four Noble Truths were simple enough: 1) that life experiences and things are not ultimately satisfying, 2) that suffering arises from attachments and desires (including the desire to avoid suffering), 3) that cessation of desire ends suffering and the cycle of rebirth, and that 4) the path of liberation can be found via the Noble Eightfold Path . . . all that was clear.

But then I got hung up on following the rules of the Eightfold Path.

I had no idea what "Right View" (the first path) was. So I started studying quantum physics to get a handle on the nature of reality, ending up in a maze of science-speak so complex with theories so mind-numbingly bizarre I didn't know which way was up.

But by God I sure felt proud of myself for studying Buddhism and quantum physics. And I worked my studies into every possible conversation just so other people would know and be just as impressed as I was!

Then I leaped over the fence into Zen Land and got hung up on Zen koans, puzzling over things like "effortless effort" and the "sound of one hand clapping." Then, trying to comprehend what union with Brahman was all about, I read (or rather started to read and quickly gave up) the Vedas and the Upanishads. Which led to other books.

What a rabbit hole!

And all the while, the silent, aware presence I AM passively waited beneath all the intellectual learning and late-night reading and puzzlement until years later I finally discovered the value in just

Simply sitting and looking within.

PRACTICE: GETTING IN TOUCH WITH I AM

Here's how simple it is.

Take a few deep breaths. Relax. When you're ready, go through the following list and say the words out loud. With every phrase you utter, notice the feelings, if any, accompanying the words. Take your time. There's no rush.

I am a human being
I am a woman/man
I am a resident of_____(state of residence)
I am a_____(name your occupation)
I am smart
I am sexy
I am happy
I am busy
I am lazy
I am an insomniac

. . . whatever you want to add.

Now take a moment and then simply say:

I am

Is there any difference in simply saying I AM versus following it with some sort of identifying tag? Say it say out loud again:

I am

Pause and sense the reverberation of those two words. Close your eyes. Tune in.

Think:

I am

Connect with the words and the feelings they evoke in your body. Or maybe there are no feelings. That's okay too. Again say or simply think:

I am

Connect with the brief silence inside your mind before all the words start rushing in to tell you how stupid this is.

Pause and rest in that silence as long as you can. Play with this as long as you like.

That's it.

10

UNITY DISGUISED

—

Who am I?
is the greatest question you can ever ask.

When Moses asked the "Who are you" question on the mountainside, God replied, *Ehyeh asher ehyeh*, "I am that I am."
How simple is that?

No descriptors. No identifying qualities. No added ingredients. Just I AM that I AM.

What would it be like to make such a response to that question? Arms wide, embracing earth and sky, head tossed back, body arched, mind and heart wide open—empty yet all-inclusive.

I am!

What an experience!

What a pure moment that would be!

No thoughts running the show. No emotions and insecurities running amok. No ego showing off. No looking over your shoulder worrying if somebody's watching. Just presence and breath and aliveness . . .

Pure Being . . .

letting the whole of Creation

rest in you

and you in it.

Now *that's* a bigger mansion!

As mystic and global humanitarian Sadhguru Jaggi Vasudev puts it: "If thought and emotion rule the nature of your life, it means you are trapped in the psychological sphere, which is essentially your own making. If you disentangle yourself from the psychological, then life and creation will happen to you in its full existential glory."

Most of us are probably seeking a moment like that . . . preferably an entire lifetime of moments like that—the naked emanation of our own being expressing through the human body without conflict, confusion, or doubt.

Simple effortless being.

I remember at a retreat one time the audience was asked to draw a picture of their greatest dream—something we each desired more than anything else in the world. There was no picture I could draw symbolizing such a moment, such a life. So I wrote the words "I AM" on the piece of paper I was given and drew a bunch of sparkly rays radiating out from the words.

At the end of the retreat we were instructed to share our pictures by spreading them out on a few tables. And I happened to overhear two young guys commenting on my picture. "What kind of stupid dream is that?" one young man said.

"I AM," said the other. "Yeah, it doesn't get dumber than that." And they moved on.

I was shocked. I mean, come on, this was a *spiritual* retreat. But later I realized they were right. To the ego, "I AM" *is* stupid. It's stupid because the ego is child of the body. It has to have dreams and desires and goals that fit the physical story. We've got to be some*thing*—an IT manager, a doctor, an astronaut. We've got to want *things*—boats, cars, iPhones, diamonds, diplomas, and PlayStations—because this is the realm of things.

Concrete, distinct, and apparently separate things.

As we will shortly see, here on Earth the brain is our real birthplace—not New York or Hong Kong. The consciousness of the immortal I AM is automatically screened out and overridden in the first few years of life by the sheer weight of physical sense perceptions we're subjected to every moment.

We're blinded by so much in this worldly realm that the body-rooted reality of I EGO becomes impregnable.

Not only do our own brains pull the wool over our eyes, the nature of the world itself disguises the integrity of I AM. How can we believe in a place of spiritual wholeness and harmony when conflict saturates earthly life? How can we possibly grasp the Oneness of I AM when the entire fabric of reality here on Earth is based in the balanced tension of opposites in a dance called polarity?

When the big bang occurred some 13.8 billion years ago, some of the very first things to coalesce into energetic "form" (which is not form at all!) were electrons and positrons. Opposing negative and positive electromagnetic forces lie at the very foundation of the multiverse.

In Creation there can be no such thing as light without dark, no up without down, no high without a low, no peak without a valley, and no way to avoid shivering with cold and baking in the heat. We get wet and dry off. We go hungry and then are filled, enjoying and disliking the sweet and sour fruits we pluck off the vine.

We love and hate, mourn and sing, stride confidently and suck our thumbs in doubt. We are healthy and sick, weak and strong, smart and stupid, rich and poor, good and bad . . . and yes, male and female.

This is how life in the material world is.

Is it so surprising then that opposition should also character- ize the ego mind, child of brain and body? Is it so surprising that creation *and* destruction characterize I EGO's journey through life and evolution?

The ego is founded in duality, not the unity I AM. And thus conflict is its nature.

We discover fire to warm ourselves . . .

and burn books, saints, and sinners.

We discover metal and shape it into plowshares . . .

and swords.

We discover a source of endless energy . . .

and a bomb to destroy all life on Earth.

We cheer as medical breakthroughs
in virology offer hope for millions . . .

then shudder in horror under
the threat of bioterrorism.

We thrill at every advance and then shake in our shoes realizing how our brilliant discoveries are consistently twisted into death-dealing mechanisms of control. And we suffer all this never once seeing the cause behind this awesome and terrible dynamic.

When are we going to recognize the source of our troubles?

When are we going to grasp the ego's perceptual matrix and the lies of separation and polarity that dictate the disastrous way I EGO functions and thinks?

How many movies do the Wachowskis have to make?

My friend Rhiannon sure never got it.

She used to point fingers at the people running the governments and corporate interests on this planet, calling them (among other things) untrustworthy, power-mad bastards. But she never saw that the same untrustworthy perceptions and dynamics were at work in her.

She wasn't willing to look in the mirror and get a handle on her own ego matrix and grow beyond it. Despite her talents, intelligence, and spirituality, her ego mind was out of control. She took all its programmed beliefs and polarized opinions deadly seriously—so much so that (as she confessed to me one day) the many conflicting inner voices often drove her to near madness.

If we take emotions and epigenetics (the study of various chemical factors influencing DNA, including the "molecules of emotion"[1]) seriously; if we adhere to the reality of a mind-body connection and accept that stress and negative thoughts and emotions can be detrimental to the health of the human body, is it too far of a stretch to entertain the possibility that it was the continuous torment of my friend's ego mind and the unhappy emotions it constantly triggered that eventually led to her final illness?

Which reminds me of a story.

I ONCE ATTENDED A spiritual retreat where I learned an intense breathing technique that was supposed to alter my consciousness and help me evolve.

Everybody else that November weekend seemed to be floating on ever-expanding clouds of breath and bliss. Me? The more I breathed the crazier my mind got.

You're not doing it right. You're not getting anywhere. You're a failure. Everybody else is getting it. What's wrong with you? You shouldn't be here. The person next to you is spitting all over your legs . . .

On and on my mind raged.

During the retreat I was invited to join a few of my fellow participants at Thanksgiving dinner in the San Juan Islands, north of Seattle. I almost said no. Thanksgiving was four days after the retreat and I had a long drive home. But I was so depressed that I agreed to go.

With time on my hands, camping gear and food in my van, and a "make it or break it" mood pushing me, I drove to a nearby state park to camp. For the three days following the retreat I sat on my sleeping bag and engaged the breath work I'd just been taught. And the crowd in my head, already tweaked by the retreat, went wild.

My parents and grandparents, the nuns, my lovers, my ex-husbands, my neighbors, my dog—all of them marched through my head with something awful to say.

It felt like my brain was going to explode. I felt like Laocoön wrestling the mighty snakes Apollo sent to plague him for trying to expose the real purpose of the Trojan Horse to King Priam of Troy.

Fortunately there were no other campers around to get spooked by the noises coming from the van. In between breathing sessions I took long walks along the Puget Sound shoreline and visited the park bathroom, sloshing water on the few parts of my body I dared expose to the cold.

The night of the third day I sat in the freezing dark, sweat running down my body from the exertion of the breath work, snot running down my face from the tears, rain beating on the metal roof of the van. And suddenly, in one of those *aha* moments, I understood my ego.

I got its whole plan.

I grasped its goal in life.

I saw what it had never allowed me to see before.

My ego wanted me dead.

What?

That's crazy! Why?

Listen . . . I kid you not. The ego may be crazy, but it has its own peculiar logic. The reason my ego wanted me dead was because:

Death is the ultimate testimony to the ego's reality as an individual "person."

Death doesn't exist for I AM.

For humans who have tapped into the silent presence of I AM and evolved beyond being driven by body-based needs and fears into transpersonal or transcendent mind-sets, death is a ridiculous concept because nonphysical awareness never dies. At that point eternal life *as consciousness itself* beyond the body beckons and death of the ego is on the horizon. *And the ego unconsciously knows this.*

The ego has a LOT invested in keeping its illusory nature

a secret—nothing less than its very existence. And weird and twisted as this might seem, for the ego identity that arises from the body and perishes with it, death is the ultimate proof of its own separated life.

"You think I'm an illusion? Well, *thbpbpthpt*! I am too real. I'm so real I'm dead. So there!"

Yes, a crazy person was indeed running my life.

But is this any different from the rest our world?

More than 99 percent of all scientists warn about the devastating impact of fossil fuels and climate change and the cataclysm the world is rapidly headed toward. But the egos in charge—the captains of government and industry crazed by their lust for personal power and control at all costs—don't give a shit.

And if the rest of us don't catch on, shift gears, and boot the crazies out of the driver's seat—including the crazy running our own lives—we already know the outcome.

Since 1950 no fewer than 263 movies depicting apocalyptic wasteland realities have hit the silver screen: *On the Beach*, *The Day the Earth Stood Still*, *Mad Max*, *Soylent Green*, The Terminator movies, *Armageddon*, *World War Z*, *Cloud Atlas*, *Wall-E* . . .

And how about the gritty visions of corporate-owned futures like *Total Recall*, *District Nine*, and *Avatar*? Or the dark views of the future that movies like *Blade Runner*, *A Clockwork Orange*, *V for Vendetta*, and *The Fifth Element* show us?

Bleak, dark, barren, stripped of all things green and growing, rapierlike skyscrapers piercing the sky, deadened enslaved souls walking slick streets, corporate messaging blazoned on every reflective surface . . . no joy, no hope, no life.

This is the future the ego desires *because death is the future the ego is equal to creating because the ego is born of the body and dies with the body.* And the Bible says it plainly:

The wages of sin is death.

—Romans 6:23 KJV

But what is "sin"?

Do we want the ego version or something closer to the truth?

The ego version means an immoral transgression against God's law. But what is God's law? Is it the ego version of God's law, which means a projection of the body-based ego's limited understanding onto the divine? Or does it mean something vaster and less structured and less physically oriented?

Originally the word "sin" was an archery term meaning "to miss the mark." And indeed, perceiving the world and self and God through the eyes of the personal ego is to miss the mark completely. In contrast:

And whosoever liveth and believeth in me [I AM] shall never die.

—John 11:26 KJV

The time of the childish ego—whose motto is "whoever dies with the most toys wins"—has had its day. Developing a vaster transpersonal, transego view is our salvation and the next step in the evolution of human consciousness.

So let's get on with seeing how we can change the channel. To accomplish this, before anything else, we need to fully understand how the ego is born. And that's what part 3 is all about.

PRACTICE: THE REALITY TO WHICH THE EGO IS EQUAL

Pop some popcorn, put your feet up, and watch one (or more) of the films I just mentioned; they're all a good bet.

If we don't catch on to the ego's act in time and stop prioritizing all the wrong things, the realities depicted in these films are what our children and their children will be dealing with.

Seriously.

So . . . I'm going to ask you a really important question:

Have you set aside that one hour a day for yourself yet? That one hour a day for going within and doing this work and thinking about this stuff and making evolutionary change within you happen?

I'm not trying to lay on a guilt trip. There's no finger pointing happening here. That's all just ego stuff anyway. I'm simply asking: Have you taken that one hour a day for yourself yet?

Have you made that a priority?

If you haven't . . . why not? What could possibly be more important?

What is steering you away from making the time to set yourself free?

Hint: The answer starts with the letter "E."

Ego Mechanics 101

11

THE EGO MAKES
ITS ENTRANCE

—

Little children have no trouble being joyful
because they haven't yet learned from outside sources
what they're supposed to be.

When my ego really started to solidify I remember wondering what it was.

I was seventeen, writing in my journal about the strange intangible film that seemed to be descending over everything, distancing me from . . . me. Separating me from life.

It was vague, but disturbing enough to write about and ponder. I actually wondered if this "distancing" was what adulthood was all about. For example, when I saw a flower, I was no longer like a little child, simply seeing a flower. Increasingly there was a "veil" between me and the flower—a veil comprised of all the things I now knew about flowers: my awareness of pollen and hay fever ads on TV; all the work entailed in planting and tending flowers in the garden; and the time I expected a corsage but my date forgot to buy me one.

Seeing a flower was no longer an act of pure presence and

perception. Now instead of engaging the flower, I was engaging my *past* and all the mental associations called "knowledge" that were telling me *about* the flower.[1]

Yikes!

I was no longer the direct experiencer of life.

I was a mental case—living with an unstoppable stream of information in my head associated with everything I saw around me—a stream of information that now kept me from flopping on the ground in the tall grasses and staring up at the clouds floating by like I unthinkingly used to do.

Now there were mental concerns surrounding everything.

Was the grass wet? Would I stain my new pants? Were there ants? What time was it? Did I close the grain bin doors in the horse barn? What was that annoying tree doing blocking that part of my view?

Listening to music, I was no longer able to crawl inside the sound and be swept away. Now I was kept *outside* the music by thoughts of how loud it was, or too soft, or the fact that I didn't like the next passage coming up.

What the hell was going on?

I didn't know anything about consciousness. I didn't have a clue about brain function and how the brain organizes and associates information, building a neurological network of knowledge enabling me to operate more efficiently in the world.

All I knew was that I had lost my ability to simply *be* in the world.

I'd lost a precious gift I didn't even know I'd had until it was now almost beyond reach. And I mourned its passing in writing, anxiously peering ahead into the unknown and my entry into the strangely convoluted new landscape called adulthood.

I was the uncertain owner of an ever-strengthening ego that would soon own me.

And Jesus called a little child unto him, and set him
in the midst of them, and said, Verily I say unto you,
Except ye be converted, and become as little children, ye
shall not enter into the kingdom of heaven.

—MATHEW 18:2 KJV

Translation: The ego is an associative information matrix of enormous complexity that grows over time until it literally *possesses* us. Eventually we see only what the ego matrix contains. The eyes of the child simply see.

PRACTICE: THE EYES OF A CHILD

Everything about the process of moving into transpersonal consciousness is about paying attention—about mindfulness. And children are wonderful windows into I AM.

They're also a great way to witness how the ego develops. Anybody with kids knows the difference between that beautiful, silent, wide-eyed presence that simply shines, blowing open the gates of your heart, and the raging little beastie who has to have his way!

1) As you go about your daily life, stay open to the observation of children. If you have none handy, in some of your contemplation time recall your own early childhood. Close your eyes and see if you can tap into the old simplicity and carefreeness.

2) When you look at something, try to consciously *see* it. Practice having fresh eyes untainted by your past experience, busyness, and the ennui of adulthood.

3) Look at a child or a picture of a little child. So sweet. So present. So beautiful! Feel the warmth in your heart that that little face and those shining eyes evoke. Feel their openness. Bask in it. Let yourself smile. Let that simplicity—the joy for no reason that is the hallmark of I AM—be yours once more.

12

BODIES "R" US

—

Welcome to the hall of mirrors . . .

The ego tells us a lot of things about the world and ourselves. But that doesn't mean what the ego says is true. Here's a classic example:

My first spiritual mentor was a meteorologist at the CBS affiliate station in Atlanta where I worked. One day, as I was editing a car commercial, he walked up and whispered in my ear, "You're not what you think you are. You're what you think."

Huh?

It didn't take but a moment's self-reflection to get clear what I truly thought I was: smart, funny, sexy, talented, athletic, competitive, deep thinking, kind, philosophic, and (since I'd just started meditating) also deeply spiritual.

Satisfied with the mental summary of my qualities, I tackled the second part of his statement and spent the rest of that day at work and the commute home watching my thoughts:

I'm hungry . . . Damn! I'm outta dog food! . . . Maybe I'll pick up some sushi . . . How am I going to buy that kayak? . . . Should

I take that freelance job? . . . I wonder if Jim wants to come over tonight . . . Did I wash that black negligee? . . . God, I can't believe what Janet said, she's such a bitch . . . I'm hungry . . . Maybe I'll get a couple of steaks . . . Maybe Jim and I can . . . Oh my! *We haven't done that in a long time!*

By the time I got home I was in shock.

And I didn't call Jim.

Had I thought I was smart and funny? My mind was a trash can and most of my humor was cutting and suggestive. Did I think I was a kind person? Then why did I think such ugly thoughts about others? If I thought I was deeply spiritual and philosophically advanced, then why was my mind consumed with sex, money, food, what other people said, and TV drama plots?

It was an enormous wake-up call, and the very first roundhouse kick to my ego. And yet it took me ages to understand that my mind was consumed with thoughts like these because *those were the things that concerned me most.*

Sure, what interested me was spirituality and lots of high-minded ideals—but the thoughts that *consumed* me related to the thing I most identified with:

My body.

I can't stress enough how body oriented we are. Our bodies and how we feel at any given moment shape our thoughts and actions and thus our lives. A simple headache can ruin everything.

When we perceive that things are going smoothly—if the boss compliments us and the scales are down three pounds that morning; if we see a flattering picture of ourselves on Facebook and eat a bowl of pasta at lunch and we're all mellowed out on the dopamine release—we feel good. And our thoughts then *reflect* this contented physical state.

We think happy, contented thoughts.

Our bodies are designed to resonate to and *reflect* our thoughts chemically. Thus our happy thoughts are amplified by more matching chemical happy feelings that in turn stimulate more happy thoughts that in turn trigger the release of even more dopamine and serotonin and we feel better and better.[1]

Euphoric, even!

By 3 P.M., you might decide to call your partner and suggest a night out. You both cuddle at the restaurant over martinis. The alcohol and oxytocin kick in. You eat a fine meal and float home, make love, and go to sleep.

Now *that* was a good day.

On the other hand, if the scale is up three pounds and the boss caught errors on a report; if it's a bad hair day, traffic was slow, and you have heartburn after lunch and feel like crap, then life and your thoughts and your resulting emotions about life suck.

And the chances of having a great evening again are now . . . ?

Zilch.

Sound familiar?

SO WHAT DOES ALL this mean?

It means that despite what many of us would like to think to the contrary, the sum total of "self" at this stage in human evolution is still pretty much:

1) A body.
2) An ego matrix of thoughts arising from the body's brain

comprising (frequently inaccurate) opinions about self and the world.

3) Concerns about maintaining this self-image.

4) An earnest (mostly unconscious) desire to maintain the comfort, security, pleasure, and amusement of this body-based "self."

Ouch!

Yes, of course, there is a *lot* more to us than that.

We feel a tremendous yearning to be more because there is so much more to be! We're taught in church to believe we're also spirit. And most of us have had experiences that show us this is true. In our heart and soul most of us know the unseen part of us is where our authentic self lies. *But because our minds are programmed by and consumed with body perceptions, we usually don't think or act as if this were true.*

Yes, we read spiritual books. Or philosophy. Or political theory. We volunteer at the animal shelter. We meditate or pray. We go to seminars. We sponsor children in Afghanistan and send money to build schools. We're good people and all this is wonderful.

But if we're honest and spend time genuinely assessing our actual moment-to-moment thoughts and the time spent on the majority of our activities (remember Sally Jane from Tallahassee!), most of us find that the thing we call "self" is highly focused on, absorbed with, and dominated by numbers one through four above.

Doggone it!

Which is why Western culture is an ego culture obsessed with sex, food, clothes, and looking good.

It's why most of us are still terrified of death. If we genuinely *knew* we were spirit as well as flesh it wouldn't freak us out as much—or at all.

Even spirituality and religion are both highly body oriented.

Since the rise in popularity of the Law of Attraction, a heavy emphasis on spiritual materialism has evolved. "Spiritual people" are as fixated on manifesting things that the body-based self wants and enjoys as everybody else.

And what about all the ancient religious rules about body maintenance and all the "unclean" foods we're not supposed to eat and how we're supposed to cook things and the specific oils and clothes and coverings we're supposed to use and wear? How about the emphasis on taming the body's animal urges?

Why do we do all this?

Well, you say, we do it in order to become more "spiritual."

But here's my point:

You cannot possibly get "more spiritual"

than you are right now, just as you are.

Everything is spirit, the body included. Hell, the body isn't even really physical.

Physics reveals (as we will soon see) that everything is actually intangible *energy* that can also be understood as *pure information* and *consciousness* itself.

But the ego mind that arises directly from the perceptions of reality our body's senses give us tells us otherwise. The body's senses tell us we are physical. The body's senses tell us we are separate and individual and alone in these fleshly shells. And the mind that arises *through the body* automatically aligns with this inescapable viewpoint.

Yes, proper study and diet and nutrition and certain practices like meditation help us advance in consciousness. But we're starting our quest from a distorted point of view that tells us we've got to become spiritual or become more spiritual. Which directly implies that we really don't know we're spirit at all.

How did we get to this place?

How did we come to believe we are that which we are *not* (physical)?

How did we become blind to what we really are (spirit/ consciousness)?

Stay tuned. The next two chapters—the most nitty-gritty and important chapters in this whole book—explain exactly how it happens.

PRACTICE: WHAT YOU THINK YOU ARE VERSUS . . .

We've done the "who" question. Now it's time to ask yourself, "What do I think I am?"

Be terrifyingly honest in your self-assessment.

Jot down the answers. Nobody has to see them.

Now, spend a few days watching your thoughts.

Are your everyday thoughts aligned with your self-image?

Or, as there was with me, is there a disconnect?

If there's a disconnect between your self-image and your actual thoughts and actions, don't despair. You're in good company. The great thing about this exercise is that your thoughts— if you really pay attention to them—will clearly reveal your ego and its main concerns and issues.

And *that* is amazing progress and a wonderful thing to learn!

Remember, you've got to know where you really are before you can get someplace else.

13

HOW THE EGO IS BORN, OR, WHERE THE RUBBER HITS THE ROAD

———

The body is the vessel for consciousness.
It's the flowerpot and the dirt the ego grows in.

Do you remember the first time you saw a dog? Heard a bird sing? Tasted an apricot? Felt the pinch of that first pair of shoes?

Most of us don't.

The first few months of life are a hurricane of undifferentiated, all-consuming physical sensations entering the brain. Life is *all* about the body.

body body body

Very rapidly, visual, auditory, and kinesthetic repetition enable the body's brain to sort things out, telling us what's what. And the first major what's what we unconsciously learn is the apparent fact that there's a "me" and something "other than me" in the world.

Separation and distinction

are the first unconscious lessons of physical life.

Our baby fingers, eyes, ears, mouth, and nose tell us the crib blanket is not "me." Our senses tell us the warm milky breast is "not me" but rather something *other* that we want and must scream for.

In the early months our brains work overtime figuring out how to induce that which is obviously outside of ourselves to respond to our body's needs for food and the elimination of discomfort caused by thirst, hunger, poopy diapers, isolation, cold, uncertainty, and everything else that life in a body bestows upon us.

Unconsciously, we learn rhythm and timing and certain associations.

We discover that activity and food happen to us in the light.

Loneliness and hunger happen while we're in the dark.

By six months we've developed a sense of agency and know we can do things to directly manipulate the outside world, like grab stuff and knock things over. Gradually the brain/body consciousness learns to navigate the physical world, differentiating and dividing, categorizing and subdividing, feeling its way, learning about the world through physical perception and repetition.

The existence of opposites is another major lesson. Left/right, big/small, in/out, wide/narrow, sweet/sour, black/white . . . The reality of physical opposites is another one of our first unconscious lessons about the world.

We discover the sky is up and the earth is down. The kitchen floor is hard. The crib is soft. On the basis of pleasant versus unpleasant body sensations, unconscious preferences are made.

Physical pleasure becomes associated with good. Pain becomes associated with bad. If we're good we get a sweet. If we're bad we get reprimanded, or worse, we get something taken away from us.

Consequences are another unconscious lesson.

We discover *if* this, *then* that.

If I slide down the stairs on my butt, *then* I don't fall. If I cry, someone will pick me up and feed me. Or perhaps I learn a harsher lesson: If I cry, no one will pick me up. Or I get punished.

We learn to mimic.

The big beings outside of us make consistent noises. We make noises back and respond to the physical cues of approval and disapproval, learning through a process of positive and negative reinforcement which responses are right and which are wrong, two more lessons in our repertoire.

If *Da* is directed to the rough-skinned being, everybody claps. If *Ma* is directed at the soft-skinned being, she hugs me in delight.

Our brains work hard to shape and sort the data—a relentless tidal wave of sights, sounds, colors, tastes, smells, and other body signals that, according to information theorists, stream into our brains at *eleven million bits of sensory data per second.*[1]

Wow! Talk about overload!

Out of necessity, a filtration system is gradually created by the brain, enabling us to deal with the sensory onslaught. All on its own our brain learns to squeeze the eleven-million-bit tsunami down to a manageable forty bits to a maximum sixty bits of data per second to make conscious cognitive processing possible.[2]

Please stop and think about this for a moment.

Throughout life we receive approximately

Eleven million bits of information per second about the world around us.

And what we consciously process is an average of fifty bits per second.

That's a *lot* of film on the cutting-room floor.

But the unconscious filtering of data via what is called the sensory gating system is a necessary fact of physical life. If for some reason the gating system residing in neurotransmitters, receptor systems, and the prefrontal cortex doesn't develop properly and the sensory tide can't be managed, cognitive function has to develop under a condition of unremitting sensory overload . . . and autism and other cognitive difficulties are often the result.[3]

Learning can be painfully slow and social interaction difficult or impossible.

If the unconscious sensory gate management system is successfully installed, we can get on with learning and interacting with the world very rapidly.

At birth, human babies have about a hundred billion nerve cells or neurons in their brains that are largely undifferentiated and untargeted. By age three a single neuron might connect with a thousand other neurons and the child's brain will have a massive neurological network of more than a hundred trillion connections and associations—a neurological network that fires a growing picture of "reality" with each new experience.[4]

Ooooo soft fuzzy orange thing. (I maul the cat and it scratches me. I scream in shock and cry.) *Soft fuzzy orange thing hurt!*

Thus I learn to leave the cat alone—or at least to treat it with caution.

One interaction at a time with cats and dogs, strained peas and bathroom potties, bikes and other tykes—this is how the neurological matrix of self and reality is constructed. An information matrix that rarely changes later in life.

Yes, the brain is incredibly plastic and neural connections can be changed and augmented at any time in life. Someday as an adult I might learn to modify some of this early unconscious behavioral programming and get past being afraid to cry and show emotion lest I be punished or ignored. Psychotherapy is good for that sort of thing.

And I'll probably end up liking cats.

But the perception of otherness, separation, distance, distinctions, opposites, and the opposing forces of pain and pleasure? All these things form the rock-bottom foundation of a learned/programmed neurological network in the brain that gives you and me our sense of "reality."

They're hardwired and not going anywhere.

SO . . . IF OUR BRAINS receive eleven million bits of information per second and then (as information theorists describe it) trigger "data compression" down to a manageable fifty bits per second, what happens to the other 10,999,950 bits of data our brain's sensory gating system boots to the sidelines every second of every day of our lives?

Granted, something has to go so we can function. But why those particular bits? What kind of information do those sidelined bits contain?

Logically, the data given the most attention by our baby brains is data relevant to navigating and manipulating the physical world to best survive and get what we want. Which is why I say our ego sense of self is grounded in a physical consciousness from the very start. Extraneous, nonphysical (psychic) information apparently ceases to register eventually because it is subtle and not as vital to direct physical survival.

Thus we end up perceiving reality through a highly physical lens. We naturally think in terms of the body until the day we die.

And this is the mind that ends up thinking

we need to become "spiritual."

BUT LET'S GET BACK to those 10,999,950 other bits of data.

In 2007, if all the world's computers were linked together, this gigantic supercomputer could carry out 6.4×10^{18} instructions per second—roughly the maximum number of nerve impulses conducted by *one* human brain *every* second.[5]

Each one of us is lugging around a three-pound supercomputer on our shoulders. Is it possible that vast amounts of subtle interdimensional data streaming into these supercomputers nonstop every second get tossed into the trash folder as not "pertinent to physical life on planet Earth"?

Is it possible that subtle realms of psychic information—the realms of angels and spirits and the interconnected dance of energy that unites everything—is it possible they form part of the "useless nonphysical information" filtered out by our brains as we mature?

How many of us beyond the age of four or five have past-life memories?

The ability to see fairies, ghosts, and angels?

Most of us can no longer perceive any of these things. There are no studies to prove that sensory gating and neurological processes such as synaptic withering and axon pruning—processes by which the brain gets rid of unused pathways and connections—are the reason people usually can't perceive these things past a certain age. But it sure makes sense.

The spirit world vanishes—not from existence,

but from our perception.

And then, as if that weren't enough, the adults around us with *their* sensory gating systems firmly intact finish the programming job our own brains start.

"There's no such thing as fairies, Alice. Stop pretending and grow up."

"There's nothing under your bed, Charlie. Go to sleep!"

"No, no darling. Grandpa's in heaven. Remember? He can't be in his chair in the living room. I know you miss him. But it's just your imagination."

Once the brain flips the switch to conform to this "seeing is believing" world, the harder it gets to regain our spiritual vision later in life. And by "spiritual" I mean the unseen, intangible aspects of existence that many people struggle to even have faith exist.

Maybe this is why so many of us have to lean on faith in the first place.

Brain function, overwhelming physical perceptions and processes, early childhood programming, the rise of the Age of Reason, modern scientific skepticism, our materialistic society, our fact-based educational system—everything seems to have conspired to remove spirit from easy reach. Pure awareness—our spiritual essence, I AM—is dulled to the point we can't sense it anymore.

Which leaves us in a really scary and vulnerable position.

Where lies our internal compass?

Where is the GPS that can guide us when all we're left with is the ego matrix arising from the body—a limited picture of reality where everything is *other* and alien, where nothing is stable or secure, where everything is changeable and therefore unreliable, where perception varies depending on point of view?

Talk about anxiety!

In a body-based world, every institution that's supposed to provide us guidance—religion, politics, business, and education—*is a creation of the physically based ego.*

Thus even at the highest levels people say one thing and mean and do another. Trust is violated. Personal agendas supersede the welfare of the whole. Priests molest children. Corporations destroy the Earth for profit. Politicians pursue money and power. Consensus is almost impossible to reach. Conflict is the global norm.

It's a reality that never seems to change.

But how can it change?

Every member of the human race is unconsciously programmed by his or her brain into believing they are physical stand-alone units, isolated and separate, fending for themselves in a harsh, physical world.

Every member of the human race is unconsciously programmed by his or her brain into believing they are physical, stand-alone units.

Every member of the human race is unconsciously programmed by his or her brain into believing they are isolated and separate.

Every member of the human race is unconsciously programmed by his or her brain into believing they must fend for themselves in a harsh, physical world.

Every member of the human race is unconsciously programmed by his or her brain into believing there is no other reality or way to be in the world.

SPIRIT BE DAMNED . . .

UNTIL WE REALIZE WHAT'S GOING ON

AND EXPAND OUR PERCEPTIONS,

EVERY SINGLE MEMBER OF THE HUMAN RACE

WILL BE CONDEMNED TO LIVE LIFE

FROM THE UNCONSCIOUS PERSPECTIVE OF A

FIFTEEN-MONTH-OLD CHILD.[6]

AND WE ALREADY KNOW THE KIND OF WORLD

THAT CREATES.

PRACTICE: REREAD THIS CHAPTER

Seriously, reread this chapter. Reread as many times as necessary to really get what it's telling you about who and what you think you are and what constitutes reality.

14

I THINK, THEREFORE I AM

—

I AM
the one irreducible Truth
leaves no room for philosophy
and yet supports its existence.

To bolster and secure its position, the ego has accumulated a lot of arguments for the primacy of its point of view and even its own existence. And over the centuries it's gathered support from some pretty heavy hitters. Remember the "father of modern philosophy" French philosopher René Descartes and what he had to say?

"I think, therefore I am."

His famous statement is part of a long autobiographical work that he wrote called *Discourse on the Method*, part of which is focused on trying to prove his own (ego) existence.

From the perspective of the ego Descartes' argument works. But from an expanded perspective, the "cogito," as it's referred to, doesn't so much prove the existence of the ego as it shows how the ego took charge in the first place.

And it's brilliant.

"I think, therefore I am" basically states:

I am because I think.

Right?

But which "I am" are we talking about?

Certainly not the silent presence I AM!

No no no. Descartes makes the same false assumption most humans make: He thinks his ego is real and the self-talk in his head actually means something. And thus he goes to great effort to explain the existence of his ego self through logic.

Imagine little baby René lying in his bassinet in his parents' house in La Haye en Touraine in France in 1596. Sometime in that first twelve-month period enough sensory data accumulated enabling his brain to figure out that the body it's operating is a separate entity distinct from Mommy and Daddy, the dog, and the milkmaid.

His mother rocks him to sleep whispering, "René." Relatives lean over the bassinet cooing, "René." His father swoops him into the air shouting, "René!"

The moment his brain associates the sound *René* with the little baby body, there is a handle to grasp—a subtle subconscious self-referencing point—a sound to attach to the perception of his separate existence.

I repeat: the *perception of his separate existence*, not the *reality* of a separate existence . . . the perception of one. There's a huge difference. Reality is what's real. Perception is:

Information our brains process from sensory input

that we are aware of.

And what is the first major message our body and brains unconsciously deliver?

That physical separation,

distance, boundaries, otherness, and individuality

are real facts of life.

And yet nothing in this world is actually separate and distinct from any other thing, because the world and all the rest of Creation is actually a boundless universal sea of energy with no borders. Physicists discovered this in the mid–twentieth century when they began smashing electrons and other particles in enormous accelerators. The farther down they looked for a physical foundation to the world, the more proof they found that the world isn't physical at all.

Trusting science and what quantum physics has to say about reality leaves us in a pretty shocking place:

There is no such thing as separate existence.

It's a concept our body/brain has taught us.

The *reality* of separate existence is not possible. Quantum physics proves this. But the *idea* of a separate existence—aha! That's possible! *That* matches the sensory data everybody's baby brain receives. And that's what unconsciously clicked for Descartes. Once the name René was associated with the body, the brain had a coat hanger upon which *identity* could be hung.

Words and language quickly followed, enabling him to express and concretize the perception-based *concept* of his individual self—words like "I" and "me" and "you"—because Mommy and Daddy spent time sitting on the floor with him in front of the fireplace at night making finger gestures pointing to themselves and saying the French equivalent of "me" and "you" or "Mama" and "Papa" and "René."

It's a language teaching game every parent in the world plays with their child, never realizing they're supporting the development of the illusion of the separate self by reinforcing the "reality" of the dual me-you relationship. *And there's nothing wrong with this.*

How else can a human child grow up capable of functioning in this world?

There's nothing bad about the creation and existence of the ego.

It's an inevitable and necessary mental construct that enables us to navigate our apparently physical reality. It's a tool, just like a shovel is a tool. The problem lies in the fact that nobody ever teaches us the ego is a tool and we end up identifying with it.

We never learn how to use it properly.

We stay stuck in the first five levels of Maslow's needs hierarchy thinking the ego self and its perceptions are *it*—the only reality—and we never move on.

We never learn to engage all that we really are.

We never discover I AM.

Instead, we diddle ourselves with mental games, confusion, doubt, skepticism, and philosophy. Somewhere around age forty, Descartes wrote *Discourse on the Method* and made the famous cogito statement saying, "We cannot doubt of our existence while we doubt."

Aaagggggghhhhh!

See what the ego mind does?

Like I have to *think* to know I AM?

I have to *doubt* to know I exist? Really?

Talk about mental masturbation. Here's what the cogito is really saying:

I am because I think my self (ego) into existence.

And once in control

I, ego,

have every intention of staying there.

PRACTICE: SELF AND OTHER

Take time to be alone. And yes, turn off your phone. Sit comfortably and look at something—a lamp, a table, a mug of coffee. Just sit and look at it and notice how separate it appears.

Note the sense of distance. How far away is this object?

Notice how different its material shape and form appear from your skin and body.

Notice its color and hardness or softness . . . all the things that tell you this object is different from you and *not you*.

Just sit and notice these things for a minute.

Now imagine the distinctions blurring. Imagine the boundaries between you and the object blurring. Imagine your body and the object as part of an invisible ocean of energy connecting you. Imagine you and the object extending into one another.

Come back to your normal view of things.

Look around the room.

Look at how much is apparently separate from you. Notice how much is unconsciously labeled *other* in your mind.

Your brain has been making this automatic assessment about

every person and object in your environment every waking moment of your life.

That's a lot of moments and a lot of separate things!

Again, imagine the distinctions blurring.

Imagine the boundaries between you and all the objects in the room blurring. Imagine your body and the room as part of an invisible ocean of energy connecting you. Imagine you and everything in the room extending into one another.

Imagine everything is one thing:

consciousness/information

I still use this practice to remind me of what's really real and true versus what my body and brain constantly tell me. It takes time to break down the illusion of separation that's been the unquestioned reality of our lives. It doesn't happen overnight. But if you keep at it, the payoff is a miraculous shift in consciousness that removes the sense of isolation and aloneness (and thus most fear and insecurity), replacing it with a sense of interpersonal connection, safety, and validity.

PART IV

Toward a Transpersonal Understanding of Self and Reality

WHO AM I?

—

Who am I?
Oh!
What a mystery!
I AM is who I am.
Pure existence.
Pure awareness.
Pure consciousness.
Pure boundless intelligence.
I AM life
Rolling like thunder
Gathering experiences.
How to explain something so empty and yet so full?
It's far easier to explain what I am not!
I AM not my body.
I AM not my mind.
I AM not my emotions.
I AM not my ego.
And yet . . .
In my fullness
These expressions become part of all that
I AM.

WHAT IS LIFE?

Really?
We have to ask this?
Yes! We must!
Not in a "pick it apart" way.
Not in a "let's analyze it to death" way.
We've already done that.
Look around.
Breathe deep.
Feel the breeze's caress.
Smile at the sound of children's laughter.
Inhale the smoke of burgers on the grill,
the perfume of cottonwood trees in spring
and gardenia.
Wonder at the night sky.
Walk on the beach.
Play Frisbee with the dog.
Laugh with your friends.
Raise a good glass of wine to your lips and drink.
This is life.
Its meaning lies in the living of it.
Why is this so hard to understand?

THE NATURE OF REALITY

—

Oneness is the deep message uniting all the world's religions.
But the form of religion itself is ego territory.
It's going to take the objectivity of science to get us to see
what the great mystics have been saying all along is true.

What else can we do in the face of what scientists have discovered about reality?

It's unbelievable! Fantastic!

Here's a really brief peek at the shocking things we now know—facts that change everything we believe about life and self, standing it all on its head just like Copernicus did to our view of the solar system all those many centuries ago.

If everybody in the world understood the next eight pages as well as the plot line for Harry Potter, our planet would change overnight!

———

EARLY IN THE TWENTIETH century, the unquestioned assumption that the physical universe is actually physical led to a scientific search for the elementary "point particle" upon which all life is built.

But as soon as scientists began smashing electrons and other particles in enormous accelerators, they quickly realized the foundations of the physical world weren't physical at all.

The solar-system picture of electrons and protons as tiny, solid, planetlike structures whizzing around a larger interior neutron in an atom was dead wrong. Electrons, muons, tauons, quarks, and gluons have no internal structure and no physical size. They are zero dimensional and more like *events* than things.

As if that weren't bad enough, electrons (those negatively charged particles that aren't really particles) were discovered to be both a wave and a particle *at the same time* (particle/wave duality). Electrons showed up in one form or the other depending on the experiment involved.

They were also hard to pin down.

Scientists can know a particle's velocity *or* its position, but not both at the same time. Which is like a cop clocking a car doing 150 miles per hour on the interstate, but not being able to locate it to give chase.

Another strange habit particles have is they can be in more than one place at the same time. Called "superposition," electrons and other nonparticle particles are capable of being in hundreds of places *simultaneously.*

It seems like the more physicists discover, the worse things get for those of us hoping to hold on to any sort of sense of normal "reality."

In fact, toward the end of his life when Einstein was asked what was the biggest physics question he wished could be answered before he died, he replied, "I'd be happy if I just knew what an electron really was."[1]

REALITY IS STRANGER THAN we think.

It's stranger than most people *can* think.

Scientists have been dealing with the shocking implications of quantum theory for a hundred years now. But as far as mainstream society is concerned, scientists' stupefying conclusions about life may as well not exist.

It's the same old same old as far as the ego matrix is concerned. And yet quantum physics has *amazing* things to say about reality that can free our minds from our superstitions and restrictions. Wave/particle duality casts doubt upon the very foundation of the scientific method itself: *objectivity* and the necessary separation of the scientist from the experiment.

Huh? Excuse me?

Isn't objectivity *the* Holy Grail of science?

Yes. It is. But at the subatomic levels, interaction and observation have been shown to affect and even determine experimental outcomes. Which ultimately points to the possibility that there are no such things as:

Separation and objectivity

Which blows everything out of the water.

I'm not going to get into the Copenhagen Interpretation and the wave function of particles. But taken to its logical conclusion, the Copenhagen Interpretation of quantum mechanics seems to imply that "reality"—the world as we know it—can only exist if some sort of measurement or *observation* takes place on the macro level of existence, the level where scientists and all of us more ordinary human beings operate.

In other words, it's possible that unless some agency (such as human consciousness) interferes, particles remain in a probabilistic state and never actualize into one location in particle form at all. Ultimately, reality as we experience it seems to be the result of human consciousness interfacing with the quantum levels of existence that are pure waves of energy.

"You think that's air you're breathing?" Morpheus asks Neo in their martial arts sparring scene in *The Matrix*. "Huh."

Think again.

Morpheus is trying to show Neo that everything he thinks is real is actually only *information* that the brain receives and translates into a picture called reality. Amazingly, scientists are beginning to think the same way.

The Copenhagen Interpretation isn't the only indicator that an information-based matrix of reality is what we're dealing with. Entanglement is another freaky physics conundrum pointing that way. Once particles have interacted, they become "entangled," which means forever after they affect each other's "spin" (which really isn't a spinning motion at all, but something called "angular momentum").

It's as if once two particles have kissed they become life-long pen pals. No matter how far apart they get, if scientists change the spin state of one entangled electron it's guaranteed its partner's spin state will change in the opposite direction in response.

Every time.

Instantaneously.

Even if they're a million light-years apart.

Which means either we ignore Einstein's theory of special relativity and its prohibition against faster-than-light travel for an information-bearing signal and accept that particles are somehow breaking the speed limit and communicating instantaneously across vast distances, *or* everything is somehow connected at the subatomic level.

And I mean everything.

Apparently even Jesus was aware of this situation. Remember the famous statement that got him into so much hot water with the Jewish people and the Sanhedrin? *My Father and I are One*, he said.

And so are we.

And entanglement is revealing why.

Replicated studies show that living cells can instantly communicate over distances. One of the simplest experiments involves a batch of algae cells grown in a petri dish. After a few days the cells are divided into two batches. One batch remains in the original dish and the rest of the cells are whisked away to a different laboratory.

When the original group of cells is stimulated by a low-voltage current, the separated group of cells in the lab miles away reacts in *precisely the same way, to the same degree, at the exact same instant* that the stimulated cells react to the charge. And when the separated batch is stimulated, the home team cells react instantaneously as well.[2]

What on Earth is going on?

If everything from entangled electrons to atoms to living cells is actually hooked up and intercommunicating somehow, then *connectivity* just might be the key to a whole new way of understanding the universe.

So far, the hunt for a medium of information exchange has led scientists on a merry chase cooking up vortices and waves theories, space-time twists, superstrings, and quantum foam. Even the ancient concept of the ether has been resurrected as a possible answer to entanglement. But the simplest, most elegant theories take us straight back to the matrix.

Noted English mathematical physicist Sir Roger Penrose theorizes that at the level of the Planck scale (an unfathomably small and unimaginably energetic scale at which even quantum field theory breaks down), the entire universe is actually pure, abstract *information.*

Not information in the usual sense of the term.

Penrose isn't talking about words or binary code. It's not electromagnetic waves carrying pictures or other electronic signals. Things like microwaves are positively *gigantic* compared to the Planck scale. Rather, Penrose believes the Planck scale is the *abstract realm of ideals* that Plato talked about: an intangible substrate of absolute coherence and mathematical geometry from which the physical world is derived and formed.[3]

Dr. Stuart Hameroff, anesthesiologist and consciousness studies expert, professor at the University of Arizona, and coauthor of numerous articles with Penrose, says, "We really don't know what the right answer is at this point, except to say that at that scale there's some kind of coarseness or irregularity. And what Penrose says is that this is Platonic information . . . embedded non-locally or holographically, so that all of the information is everywhere, wherever you go."[4]

American theoretical physicist David Bohm has also created a model where the entire universe and every particle in it comprises an "explicate order" resulting from active *information* contained holographically in an underlying "implicate order."

Which means that everything that exists contains the information of everything else that exists. The information of the entire universe is contained holographically in every single cell.[5]

It's hard to grasp when we're sitting in traffic or waiting in the doctor's office to get a flu shot, but science is revealing that our world is more of an *idea* than anything else.

As famous Austrian theoretical physicist Erwin Schrödinger

put it, "What we observe as material bodies and forces are nothing but shapes and variations in the structure of space. Particles are just *Schaumkommen* [appearances]."[6]

———

I USED TO LIE in bed at night for hours wondering how my hand and my pillow, the parquet tiles on the floor in my bedroom, and the sultry night air wafting over my body could all be nothing but intangible information.

How was it possible?

It was crazy! I mean, come on. This stuff is *real*!

But what is real? How do we define it? As physical beings—oops—as *apparently* physical beings, of course we would define reality in physical terms. But given the inescapable scientific proof we have now gathered, it seems this world (and everybody in it) *isn't physical at all.*

Which means this world

And me

And you

Must be something altogether different

And we just don't know it . . .

Yet.

Merrily merrily merrily merrily
Life is but a dream.
—NURSERY RHYME

Reality is merely an illusion, although a very persistent one.

—ALBERT EINSTEIN

Whether we call it the unfolding implicate/explicate order, "irregularities in the fabric of space," Planck scale information, or Platonic ideals doesn't matter. Invisible, intangible, and unfathomably powerful energies lie at the foundation of the universe, interconnecting and interpenetrating all life—unfolding *as* life.

And these energies are best understood as information/intelligence/consciousness itself.

As Swami Muktananda puts it, "The Self, Shiva is supremely pure and independent, and you can experience it constantly sparkling within your mind. It cannot be perceived by the senses, because it makes the senses function. It cannot be perceived by the mind, because it makes the mind think. Still, the Self can be known, and to know it we do not need the help of the mind or the senses."[7]

Bottom line, matter and energy, information and consciousness are just different ways of looking at the same thing. And if we include the experience of mystics who have directly grasped and taught about the unified consciousness of Creation for millennia, we can add the word "self" to this interchangeable mix as well.

SELF

=

Intelligence = Information = Energy = Mass = Life = God = Spirit = Consciousness

It's all the same thing.

It's all ONE thing.

PRACTICE: REDEFINING REALITY

When I'm driving or lying awake in bed at night, instead of trotting out the same old tired ego worries, I consciously shift gears and contemplate Bigger Things. Which is a great way to start moving into an expanded consciousness and alignment with reality as it really is.

There's a *lot* to contemplate in this book. Take notes. When you've got some downtime (which you're creating), think about this stuff. Here are a few topics to prime the pump:

> You've never actually touched anything in your entire life. Electron repulsion between your fingertips and another person's hand or a piece of clothing or a hairbrush makes touching any other thing impossible. Plus, at the subatomic level, everything is energy and nothing is really tangible anyway.
>
> What gives you the impression of touch?
>
> Why do we experience the world as tangible if it's not tangible? How is this possible?
>
> What makes something "real"? What is meant by the word?
>
> Is the world "real" if it isn't "physical"?
>
> What force or medium could possibly create and support the appearance of tangible things that are but mere *Schaumkommen* (appearances)?

THE LIVING UNIVERSE

—

The mind boggles contemplating life.
If it doesn't, you're not really contemplating life.

nomalies in cosmic background radiation detected by the Planck telescope reveal that the universe might actually be the "multi-verse." Instead of one universe it's possible there are millions of universes,[1] each one containing billions of galaxies. And even if there's only one universe, which looks unlikely, the current estimate of the number of galaxies in our universe alone is 176 billion galaxies.[2]

Whoa!

When you consider that our home base—the Milky Way galaxy—has an estimated 8.8 billion habitable planets that may contain life,[3] Creation starts getting pretty big. And let's not even get into the issue of other potential dimensions where other forms of intelligence could be hanging out.[4]

Infinite intelligence is constantly creating fathomless inter-twining multidimensional dimensions—infinite fractal realities, "wheels within wheels"—mazes of consciousness and informa-tion that go on and on and on, spinning the drama of universes and galaxies and angels and demons and aliens and heavens and hells and purgatories and rooms filled with breathlessly waiting virgins and a gazillion other stories we can't even imagine—all as "real" as consciousness can make them.

Which, as anybody who has ever stubbed their toe knows, seems pretty damn real.

Not only is Creation far vaster and more intricate and multi-layered than anything we've previously imagined, not only is everything interconnected as "one thing" at the most fundamental quantum levels, everything in Creation is also alive—even the multiverse itself.[5]

––––––––

OUR ANCIENT ANCESTORS WERE no strangers to the idea of dwelling in an alive and intelligent universe. Until Christianity forbade such pantheistic views and the rise of scientific reductionism and Newtonian physics led us toward a deadened view of the universe—seeing life as a clockwork mechanism based purely in mathematical and mechanical terms—most people saw the Earth and heavens as alive.

We walked through a living world.

Animals and plants and rocks had spirits—as did the sky and waters and stars and sun and moon. Shamans trance-danced, reaching out to the bison and buffalo with their inner vision, locating them for the hunters. Men and women carefully tended the garden of the world, making sure everything stayed in balance and that the plants and animals weren't overharvested. Hunters blessed the spirits of the animals they killed for food, giving thanks. The women blessed the spirits of the plants as they picked roots and berries and herbs.

> *And while I stood there I saw more than I can tell*
> *and I understood more than I saw;*
> *for I was seeing in a sacred manner the shapes of*
> *all things in the spirit,*
> *and the shape of all shapes as they must live together*
> *like one being.*[6]
> —BLACK ELK, OGLALA LAKOTA SIOUX

It's impossible to feel alone in a vibrant, interconnected world where the air we breathe is saturated with life and energy, and every footfall lands on soil overflowing with living beings and microorganisms. The mountains we climb, the valleys and plains we dwell upon, the rivers and lakes and seas we swim in are filled with creatures of all kinds and varieties of consciousness.

Plants communicate with one another via bioacoustics through their root systems. The rhizosphere hums with plant talk.[7] Maple trees that are attacked by insects alert other trees to ramp up their chemical defense systems.[8] Jewelweed curbs its leaf growth and elongates its branches in the presence of other jewelweed plants to give their kin more room to grow.[9]

Chimpanzees communicate with humans via sign language. Dogs have the equivalent vocabulary of a two- to three-year-old child. Dolphins and whales have a brain-size-to-body-mass ratio larger than humans and exhibit incredibly complex communication patterns.

According to David Bohm, life is enfolded in everything and implicitly present even when not manifest.[10] In the book *The Living Universe*, Duane Elgin points out that our universe exhibits all the characteristics of a living system:

1) The universe is a unified whole.
2) Energy flows through every part of the system.

3) The universe continuously regenerates itself.

4) There appears to be sentience at every level (what is called primary perception and movement toward self-awareness and perception).

5) The universe exhibits the freedom to make choices even down at the particle level.

6) The universe reproduces itself through black holes and white holes.

"We do not need to create or imagine awakening experiences," Elgin writes. "Instead, we only need to experience directly what is already true about the fundamental nature of the universe. . . . Life is constantly seeking to connect with itself—to know itself and grow itself to higher levels of self-organization."[11]

And *all* this stunning amount of activity takes place within the 4 percent of the universe we know about and can see. Yes, that's right: *4 percent.*

Dark matter and dark energy comprise a full 96 percent of our universe.

We can't see either and have no idea what they actually are. But they're there. And the implications are staggering. "If 96 percent of the known universe is invisible," says Elgin, "then how much of ourselves is invisible and not detectable by material technologies? How far do we extend into the deep ecology of the invisible universe?"[12]

How far indeed?

PRACTICE: STARGAZING AND . . .

Get out into nature as much as you possibly can, even if it's just in your own backyard or a local park. Take long walks. Drive into the country.

Look up the moon phases and pick a night when the moon is new or in an early crescent phase and plan a stargazing trip alone, with a friend, or with the whole family.

Pack a midnight snack and head out into the countryside. (It's hard doing this in the city with all the light pollution.) Spread your blanket on the ground and spend a couple of hours with the stars. If you're with people, take a bunch of blankets and let everybody have their own launch pad.

Be quiet. Leave the headphones and cell phones in the car. Listen to the night sounds. Soak in the vastness of the starry sky and imagine all the wonders it holds.

Or, pack a picnic lunch and plan a day's outing into the fields and forests or to a lake . . . by *yourself.* (*What? Oh no! I can't possibly! Leave the kids? No way!*) Yes, leave the kids and everybody else and go sit by a stream. Wade in the water. Stick your toes in the mud.

When was the last time you did this?

Peer under rocks. Isn't it amazing what's there?

Walk through the grasses. Lie on your back and watch the clouds. Breathe it all in. It's part of you . . . all of it.

Sit and watch one patch of forest floor or a small section of grassy pasture (not a chemically treated lawn!) for ten minutes. It's stunning what you'll find in just a few square feet of soil. While you're watching the ants scurry and the beetles burrow, imagine how many insects there are on Mother Earth—and then think of the stars and all their planets and all the possible interplanetary ants and beetles in existence.

MEDITATION

Find a comfortable, quiet place outside to sit. Close your eyes or keep them semiopen. Let your mind reach out.

Incorporate as much *life* as you can possibly see or imagine and *feel* it as part of you. Feel your sense of "self" expanding. How many plants and animals can you contain? How many people? How many children? How big can "you" get? How loving? How much life can you contain?

Remember there's a reason Thoreau went to Walden Pond and Jesus went into the desert: It's expansive. Being in nature relaxes, inspires, and alters brain function in a good way,[13] naturally inducing alpha waves indicative of a meditative state. On the other hand, living in urban environments is stressful to the body and mind.

I've spent many years living alone in one-room cabins without indoor plumbing out in the middle of nowhere. Radical? Maybe. But, frankly, those were some of the most amazing years of my life! Living deep in nature, saturating myself in solitude for long periods of time, was one of the smartest things I ever did. And I continue to seek both as a way to replenish mind, body, and spirit on an as-needed basis.

17

PERCEPTION IS . . . EVERYTHING

—

Seeing is believing . . . or not.

Let's pretend for a moment that the world is actually physical. Let's pretend the standard social view of reality is accurate. Let's pretend there's nothing else happening—no billions of other universes, no infinite number of dimensions, no subtle Planck scale information informing everything. Let's pretend it's business as usual down here on three-dimensional planet Earth.

And here we are, the ultimate creation: *Man!* Crowned by God himself as overlord of the domain.[1] Nothing gets past *us*. Our senses are honed. Our observations are keen. We're fine-tuned machines! We're . . .

Actually, almost blind.

Let me tell you how I discovered this.

I was sitting in a room with sixty-two other people when Marilyn Schlitz, PhD—researcher, social anthropologist, and senior scientist at the California Pacific Medical Center—gave a talk on something called "inattentional blindness and selective attention."

During the talk she played a video of six people in an office hallway rapidly passing a volleyball around the group. Three people wore white shirts and three people wore black shirts, and all of us attending the lecture were instructed to count the number of times the ball was passed between the people wearing the white shirts.

About fifteen seconds into the video I lost count and gave up the exercise. To my total shock, a big guy in a gorilla suit suddenly materialized out of nowhere, standing in the center of the people passing the ball! He faced the camera, beat his chest, then turned and walked off while the ball exercise was still in motion.

"How many of you saw something unusual in this video?" Schlitz asked a minute later when the clip finished. One other woman and I raised our hands. The sixty-one other people saw nothing out of the ordinary. When she ran the same video again, telling us to simply watch the video and not count ball passes, there the gorilla was, clear to everyone.

Audience reactions ranged from stunned to indignant, with a couple of people accusing Schlitz of playing two different videos to trick them. But who needs somebody to trick us when we trick ourselves?

The whole point of the exercise was to show people how much information humans constantly miss—*enormous* things like a freaking *gorilla* standing directly in front of a camera in a small hallway!

Which makes me wonder: If I can miss a gorilla standing in plain sight, what else am I not seeing?

So, let's stop pretending we know what's going on and see how we arrange the puny amount of information that does get through our sensory gating systems into "reality."

One way to get a visual handle on how we organize the explicate order (the external world) is a figure-ground study created in 1915 by Danish psychologist Edgar Rubin called Rubin's vase.[2]

The drawing depicts two images with a common border, in this case identical facial profiles facing one another that create another image of a white vase in between.

It doesn't matter which image you see first. Quickly, the other view asserts itself, back and forth, back and forth, white vase black profiles . . . white vase black profiles . . . our eyes perceive one form or the other.

Either this or that.

Remember, perceiving distinctions and differences is the way a baby first starts to make sense of the world. Recognizing similarities between different objects comes later. But whether I'm seeing differences or similarities doesn't matter. Pattern recognition is part of the automatic process my brain goes through as separate pieces of sensory data are organized to make sense of the world, giving me the picture of "reality."

And because my brain works this way, the larger perspective of wholeness is mostly unavailable to me. The Rubin's vase picture is *one* thing. But I can't see it because my brain gives me identifiable pieces, not the whole.

Just like life, I can't see the picture as *one*. I can only see it in terms of separation, otherness, and fragmentation.

———

SO WHAT ARE WE supposed to think when scientists and mystics tell us life is one vast, intelligent, seamless whole? How can we possibly get it?

We can't!

Not with our brains programmed to perceive Oneness in separate bits and pieces. As American philosopher Ken Wilber puts it:

To contract at all in the face of this undivided wholeness awareness, this total painting of all that is existing in this timeless all-inclusive present, is to set in motion the self-contraction, the separate self-sense that latches onto the relative, finite, conventional small self—a necessary functional entity for this manifest world created by the

True Self itself, along with the rest of creation—but latches onto that small self, or "I," as if it were itself the True Self, or "I-I," thus setting in motion the entire train of events known as ignorance, illusion, Maya, deception, the fallen world, the world of the lie.[3]

We're condemned to a world of this and that, faces and vases, me and you, living a lie of separation and fragmented appearances, all the while thinking we've got a handle on reality and know the whole truth about what's going on.

Stunning, eh?

But here's a visual that can help us put all the pieces together.

In the movie *I Heart Huckabees*, Dustin Hoffman plays existential detective Bernard Jaffe. In one scene Bernard and a young man named Albert are talking and Bernard grabs a blanket, holds it out, and tells Albert the blanket represents the universe, the fabric of all existence.

He pokes a finger up from underneath, creating a finger-shaped mound in the blanket. This, he says, is me.

He sticks more and more fingers up through the blanket, identifying some of the mounds as the Eiffel Tower, a hamburger, a war, an orgasm, and Albert.

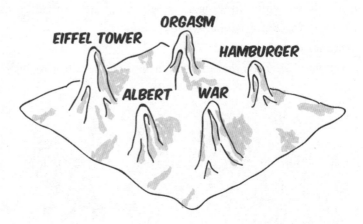

Everything in the world of physical creation *appears* individual and unique, he explains. But in reality, everything is really one thing: the blanket.

In one simple demonstration, Albert has explained Planck scale information, infinite intelligence, consciousness, I AM—God—whatever you want to call the underlying connecting substrate of existence—and how Oneness reveals itself through multiplicity.

Wow.

Don't you just love the movies?

PRACTICE: STEPPING INTO LIFE

One of the most common things I do aside from meditate, watch my mind like a hawk, and get out in nature, is consciously work at moving into the transpersonal state of consciousness. I practice seeing and being the blanket. And the Stepping into Life exercise is the practice I use to do that.

Find a quiet space to sit. Breathe calmly and relax for a minute. Then slowly look around and take in your surroundings. Don't fix your gaze on any one thing. Let your gaze relax and soften. Just look around and let the world come into you.

Now, let your gaze gently rest in one general direction.

Don't keep looking around. But don't fix your gaze either. Don't look *at* anything in particular or try to study it. This isn't about noticing stuff or looking for details. Just look toward something—a picture, a lamp, a sweater draped over a chair— and let your eyes soften to allow that object and the world around that object to enter your visual awareness.

In martial arts this diffusing of the visual senses is called "soft eyes." And it enables you to actually perceive more of what's around you, both visually and energetically.

Let your chin drop a bit so you can see some of your body as well.

Keep soft eyes and let the visual of your shoulders, your nose, your chest, your belly, your legs and feet, your arms and hands enter the picture. Don't *look* at your body. Just let it be part of the picture of the world you're in.

Sense your connection with the room or the outdoors, wherever you're sitting. Let the boundaries soften between you and the space around you. Feel yourself blending with your environment.

As the feeling deepens, sense the space behind you. Close your eyes for a few moments and feel the whole room or the world surrounding you 360 degrees.

Open your eyes.

Keep the sense of a 360-degree expanded self. Sense the truth that you are *in* the picture of life, not just watching it or separately walking through it.

Now, once again slowly look around your surroundings. Take your time. Appreciate what you see. Notice things but don't stare at them. Just notice.

Shift back into soft eyes. Gently lower your chin and shift your soft-eyed vision to once again include your body in the picture. Sense the world containing you. Sense your *inclusion*.

Maintain soft eyes and softly say:

This is what I am

Stay present and aware of yourself in the full picture of life.

Breathe.

Do this process for as long as you like.

AS YOU GET USED to doing the process, you can bring to mind other thoughts while you're in this open, inclusive space, such as:

I am *all* of life.

I am the multiverse.

I am one with all I see.

I am one with all I don't see.

Bathe in this enormous inclusive view of self. *This* is who you really are. You are everything you see and more. The multiverse is your support system.

Think it's big enough?

18

GETTING IT TOGETHER

—

As above, so below.

Right now, we humans are less like the blanket (seamlessly whole) and rather more like Scarecrow in *The Wizard of Oz* after the winged monkeys sent by the Wicked Witch of the West have taken him apart.

Not only do we see life in parts and pieces, we *live* life in parts and pieces.

We have highly developed bodies. We have a mental identity called the ego. We have emotions. And we've developed superb physical, intellectual, and relational systems based on these three aspects of our existence.

Unfortunately, these three parts of our "selves" rarely work in unison.

Our minds say one thing. Our bodies say another. Our emotions, which seem to be something altogether separate but are actually chemically created by the body in reaction to situations and our thoughts,[1] send us in yet another direction.

And then there's that vague fourth "something else"—an inner sense, the promptings of something larger and "spiritual"—

that urges us toward yet another perspective and intangible destination.

No wonder we're so easily confused and don't know what to do. How can it be any other way with all these different voices and impulses pushing and pulling for dominance with no understanding of how these aspects of "self" are supposed to come together to work as a team?

Welcome to yet one more reason why we're so horribly stuck:

Our triune nature.

THE ABRAHAMIC RELIGIONS OF Christianity, Judaism, and Islam view human beings as creatures created by God, contained within God's radiance and yet separate from him. This relationship can be pictured as a triad, with God looking down upon his human creation comprised of three elements:

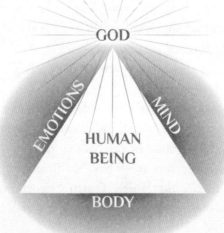

Of course, traditionally we're also seen as having a "part" of God in us as well. And the intangible aspects of the human being—soul and spirit—are often vaguely lumped together under the category of "spirit."

If we combine the body and its chemically based emotions within one leg of the triad, we come up with the following picture of our general makeup and relationship with God:

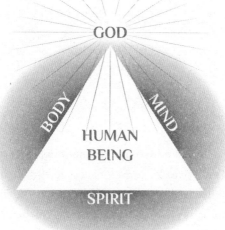

Again we are fragmented into three different components. In both views God is either something altogether separate or partially separate, while spirit is some incomprehensible, intangible "aspect" of us linking us to the divine.

But if science is right and mystics from Buddha to Jesus are right and everything is actually *one* thing, and if things are not really concrete "things" at all but rather invisible, intangible information called consciousness, then we have an entirely new way of viewing God, spirit, and ourselves. It's a less fragmented view that matches what both science and mysticism reveal:

Consciousness / I AM

Expressing via body, mind, and emotions.

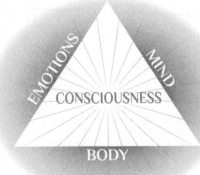

In this view, man and woman are no longer the receptacles of a "piece" of God—we are consciousness itself. We are no longer a "human being" with spirit as a part of us. We *are* spirit. We are consciousness (I AM) expressing through the *appearance* of mind/body/emotions.

SO WHERE DOES THIS leave us?

It leaves us at the point of responsibility.

It brings us to the place where we have to take a deep breath and tell ourselves, "Okay. I'm spirit, *just as I am.* No more confusion.

"Humanity is consciousness/spirit extended into bodily form on the frontier of Creation. I am consciousness with a name and a face and hands and heart and an address on planet Earth. Science and *all* the great mystics of all time tell me that everything and everyone around me is, at the most profound level, aspects of my self.

"There is something inside that tells me this is true.

"So looking around this world, I have to ask, 'Am I happy with my self?' Am I happy with all that I am and all that I see in this Creation I AM?

"And if the answer isn't a resounding *yes!* reverberating to the heavens in joy and satisfaction, then it's *my* responsibility to do something about it."

If we are all

ONE

Who else is there?

PRACTICE: SURRENDER

By doing the Stopping exercise (chapter 7), you took a *major* step toward I AM. It may seem like you were doing nothing (which is the whole point of stopping). But you were actually letting go the frantic doing that defines the ego, keeping it intact, running the show. Next we will learn the act of surrender because that's what it takes to open up to the silent I AM presence within us.

Unfortunately, "surrender" is a dirty word in the English language.

We live in a highly masculine society that is very much about getting ahead by beating out the other guy. Surrender in this world means losing. It means defeat and failure. It means giving in and giving up. It means being a wimp . . . as offensive as it sounds, a *pussy*.

And yet there is another kind of surrender.

Sexuality plays a major role in the polarity of opposites on this planet. And if we look at how the sexes generally tend to express, men tend to be the sexual aggressor—the taker—and women tend to be the one willingly surrendering, becoming the "takee."

It's a great game, and the billion-dollar-a-year romance novel industry is based on this dynamic. Strong, virile men stride across the pages, and strong, alluring women swoon, breasts heaving, into their embrace. The longing to be taken—ravished—the longing to surrender, and also the fear of it, is a large part of the romance formula. And the woman who successfully sexually surrenders wins the prize: lots of orgasms and a man who is eager to please her in other ways as well.

And if you're wondering why I'm getting into all this, please be patient and open-minded. There is another kind of surrender I want to talk about that is directly related to sexual surrender in its methodology and felt sense, and that is:

Surrender of the ego to I AM.

––––––––––

RELIGIOUS ECSTASY HAS A long and honored place in Christian history. Physical symptoms of rapture are usually seen as indicators that the Holy Spirit has "descended" upon the worthy recipient and taken him or her over. Bodily shaking, trance states, writhing, tears of joy, speaking in tongues, levitation—all are considered "normal" under these circumstances. The seventeenth-century Franciscan monk Saint Joseph of Cupertino, for example, was said to often levitate while saying Mass.

In the Eastern view, physical manifestations of spiritual rapture are thought to be due to the rush of kundalini energy (life force) rising upward from the base spinal chakra (energy center at the root of the spine) that is released once a certain level of spiritual surrender and depth of meditative union has been reached. It is most commonly witnessed on the path of bhakti yoga, the path of devotion.

As in Christian worship, in bhakti yoga God is seen as a completely external being, the object of passionate worship and adoration to which the aspirant surrenders, mind, body, and soul. Like Christianity, the aspirant may also worship the divine through the body/presence of the guru (Jesus).

Although it's usually not talked about in these terms, spiritual ecstasy includes a feeling of sexual ecstasy, and surrender to the divine has the same kind of dynamics as sexual surrender—at least for a woman. (I have no idea what sexual surrender feels like for a man. Sorry, guys! But I'm sure you'll get the sense of it as I go on.)

The reason I know spiritual and sexual surrender share the same dynamics is because in later years, deep in meditation, I'd feel a blatantly sexual rush of energy upward from my groin that would fill my entire body. The feeling was so delicious it was almost orgasmic, and I'd rock back and forth, moaning and laughing, opening myself, crying out *Beloved!* to God and the whole of Creation.

No wonder I so rarely missed morning meditation!

Union with I AM is ecstatic because I AM is ecstatic. Only the ego at lower levels of consciousness is miserable.

———

SO, LET'S GET ON to the Surrender exercise. The whole point is to get to the place where you let go and open up to receive the divine. And to prime the pump for this, it helps to get reacquainted with plain old sexual surrender. During the exercise I want you to close your eyes and imagine you and your lover in a passionate embrace. Feel the softening that occurs in your body as well as the excitement. Feel the energy rise from the sexual center at the base of your spine. Sense the letting go of the mind. Sense the yielding to passion and the "other."

No thought . . . just sensation . . . relaxing into utter pliability and receptivity . . .

Do with me as you wish . . .

Take me.

I am yours.

THIS IS THE PLACE sexual surrender takes a woman: to the delicious sense of offering herself up—lips, breasts, womb, heart, mind, soul, love—yielding to the rise of life-force energy, embracing her emptiness, yearning to be filled. And in that delicious receptive emptiness, she lets her lover (physical or divine) in.

For men, this practice might take a lot of imagination. Surrender is *not* the masculine path. When sexually excited, the male gets hard, not soft. He goes into aggressive taking mode, not yielding mode. Which is why the bhakti path of devotion is usually the path of women and the paths of karma, jnana, raja, and hatha yoga—the paths of action, logic, energy and introspection, and bodily purification—are more often pursued by men.

And if judgment bells are going off in your head about how "unspiritual" all this is, congratulations! You've just hit the ego's religious separation program dividing sexuality and sensuality from spirituality, making the body and sex "bad" and the divine "good" because it's nonphysical.

But guess what?

The body isn't actually physical either. Ha! So tell your ego that its issues and judgment about the body and sex can go take a hike.

SURRENDER EXERCISE

Sit in a comfortable position, eyes closed, and enter your fantasy. Once you're feeling pliant, excited, and open, exchange the fantasy of a physical lover for the thought of opening to the divine lover:

I am

Close your eyes, rest your hands, palms up, on your thighs. Breathe deeply while retaining the feeling of empty receptivity being filled by I AM. Feel the fullness and the energy inside.

As you feel the energy mounting say: I AM.

Don't say the words forcefully. Barely breathe the words. *Make love to the words.* Whisper them. Let them fill you with even more delight: *I AM.*

Feel the energy.

Don't try to do anything with it. Don't try to raise your kundalini energy to your crown chakra (the top of the head). Don't *do* anything except open and surrender and feel the fullness of life moving within you. If you move into physical ecstasy, that's fine. If you don't, that's fine.

Just feel presence and energy

expanding throughout your entire being.

Be filled.

Just be.

19

THE THREE MINDS

—

To know where one stands in the scheme of things—
to get even a glimpse—is a gift.

As we move into the transpersonal mind-set we become our own saviors.

The ego is tempered. Our triune nature balances. Instead of being our nemesis and torturer, the mind becomes the tool it was meant to be, helping us to accomplish all the things we want to do.

The body and its emotions no longer sway us off course. Our hearts open.

We move into greater harmony with ourselves and thus with others and life. Oneness becomes a lifestyle, not a philosophy. We are naturally kinder and more giving, concerned for the welfare of all people and other life forms, including our planetary home.

The transpersonal man or woman is not necessarily experiencing unity consciousness. They may have no idea such a consciousness exists. They are simply aware of the brotherhood and sisterhood of life and the need for taking care of both self and others.

This is the stage where we finally accept our role as stewards of the Earth.

Many millions of people are in, or are entering, this stage. In fact, more than eighty million people in the United States and 120 million people in Europe are part of what is now called the LOHAS demographic—the Lifestyles of Health and Sustainability.[1] These are the people driving the environmental movement, the alternative health movement, and the sustainability movement in business, socioeconomics, and agriculture. Each individual in this demographic is an example of our growing evolution into transpersonal territory.

And yet there is another step we will eventually take: the transition from transpersonal to transcendent consciousness, where we go beyond the personal and the physical altogether and move into the consciousness of Oneness itself.

The allegory of the blanket is one way we can get a visual handle on our progression through the three mind-sets of 1) personal ego, 2) the transpersonal self, and 3) transcendent consciousness.

Let's say each peak of the blanket represents an individual person. The personal ego hates the idea of the blanket. It doesn't accept that every peak is a precious and unique expression of I AM that is not lessened by realizing it shares the absolute *sameness* of its divine nature with every other peak. It perceives that with Oneness its uniqueness and specialness disappear.

Coming from the personal ego perspective, one peak sees another peak and sees nothing connecting the two. The two peaks are in competition over resources and will probably go to war to prove who is the bigger peak in order to win supremacy and feel secure in their isolation.

Fortunately, as the narrow view of the ego expands into transpersonal territory, we are no longer consumed with the fears that arise from the personal ego's need for specialness and separation. Instead of struggling in competitive isolation, we begin to experience a reality where the whole of life itself becomes our support system.

Which means our potential as an individual "peak" expressing life

has just exploded to encompass

everything.

In the transpersonal state of mind, one peak sees another peak and recognizes it as being either like itself or even genuinely *as* itself. Cooperation is natural and effortless. It is at this point in evolution that the deepest, most mysterious paradox of human existence, multiplicity within Oneness, begins to resolve.

Closure on the paradox happens at the level of transcendence. The transcendent peak sees only the blanket.

Please understand this is only a metaphor using the blanket as a visual representation. An enlightened being is perfectly capable of seeing the either/or aspects of life and the parts and pieces of the picture. It's just that in transcendent consciousness the illusion of individual self as a reality is dissolved.

The enlightened being is no longer an individual human.

In fact, an enlightened being is no longer a human being at all. He or she might *look* human to outside eyes. But the human is long gone.

There is only I AM.

———

ALBERT EINSTEIN ONCE SAID, "The formulation of the problem is often more essential than its solution." And such is the case with evolving consciousness.

Once you know that *all* the systemic problems in your life, the lives of those around you, and the lives of everyone else on the planet are the result of the unrecognized personal ego running amok—an erroneous body-based point of view we call "self" that isn't really self at all—your path to living a greater life is clear.

If you're contemplating this whole subject of the ego and taking it seriously, if you're beginning to scrutinize your life and thoughts and actions in light of what this book is saying . . . if you haven't just read the words and thought, "Gee, that's interesting. What's for dinner?" and then picked up the next hot thing to try to find the answers to your troubles . . . then I daresay the solution to your troubles is well on its way because:

If you do the work and genuinely see the ego for what it is,

everything changes of its own accord.

Things can't help but change, because if you've genuinely grasped what the ego is *your consciousness has already shifted*.

And that's all I AM needs to move mountains.

PRACTICE: SYNTHESIS

The Stopping practice, which you learned in chapter 7, and the Surrender practice, which you learned in the last chapter, are the first two steps in what I call the embodying wholeness process, which teaches us how to *embody* the consciousness I AM (which, of course, you already do—just not consciously!).

The last step of this process is synthesis, and it's kind of hard to describe. But imagine yourself in the fullness of embrace with I AM as your divine lover. Or imagine yourself in your physical lover's embrace.

You're filled up, right? No parts are missing. There is no yearning. You're simply richly, satisfyingly *complete*. The final step is to embrace divine consciousness *as* yourself instead of embracing the divine lover. This embodiment of the divine is what I call synthesis.

So how do you shift the completeness you experience surrendering to the divine lover into a sense of being the divine itself? And then how do you shift this embodiment from the meditation pillow out into your day-to-day life, and also maintain it?

Here's how I did it: In the moments moving into union with the divine Beloved in meditation:

I stopped focusing on the other.

When the energy would rise and my body was suffused with sweetness, instead of crying out to the Beloved outside of me—I AM—to fill me, I brought myself into the picture, exactly as the Stepping into Life exercise (pages 131–33) outlines.

I opened my arms wide and then brought them into my chest and hugged *myself*, whispering "Beloved," including myself in the honoring, including myself as divine lover, rocking myself, sometimes eyes open, sometimes eyes closed, whispering:

Beloved!

Me

You

Everything One

I am

Synthesis is the place beyond union—the place where there are no longer two forces in existence melding together in wholeness. It is I AM—the place where the illusion of division (and thus the yearning for wholeness) never occurred and doesn't exist.

Eventually I only had to remember the truth: *I AM*—and recall the *feeling* of synthesis I consciously evoked during my meditations. It didn't matter where I was, driving my car or working on the computer or walking in a shopping mall. With just a thought, I could step into the sense of being I AM and hold it.

Bodies are great this way. Just as a hypnotherapist gives a client a cue word that instantly induces a state of relaxation after they've learned how to relax, the same is true of the embodying wholeness process. Once the *feeling* of synthesis has been consciously noted, it can be instantly engendered by thought alone.

So let's put it all together, shall we?

EMBODYING WHOLENESS PROCESS

1) Stop!
   There is no way to leapfrog from ego to I AM consciousness
   while still indulging the ego's agenda. You have to take the time
   and stop doing what you usually do to make room for something greater. After you've actually learned to stop and can sit
   quietly in silence for a half hour or more without your head
   feeling like it will explode, you're ready for the whole process.
   So Stop! Get into a relaxed and receptive space, and then:

2) Surrender
   Close your eyes and go into your sexual fantasy. At the point
   of feeling open and pliant, ready to receive your lover, switch
   from a physical lover to imagining the divine lover I AM
   taking you and sweeping you away. Revel in the completeness of feeling filled up with the divine.

3) Synthesis
   Dissolve any sense of surrendering *to* something outside you.
   Step into the picture. Embrace your own being as divine.
   Dissolve the sense of twoness. Be the One—I AM.

After you've learned to stop and learned to surrender to I AM
and then practiced synergy by putting yourself in the picture *as*
the Beloved over and over and over again, eventually it becomes
automatic.

Then all you have to do is think or whisper I AM and . . .

Whoosh!!

The Spiritual Ego and Enlightenment

BEFORE WE MOVE ON . . .

—

Congratulations.

You've made it through the sections about the ego
and how to evolve your mind to transpersonal awareness.
This is no small feat. Pat yourself on your apparently
physical back and let all this information sink in.

Practice the practices.

They may seem simple, and they are. But this is not
an "I did it once, what's next?" kind of thing.

*Changing consciousness is a process,
and repetition and consistency are the great tools
that make it stick.*

I highly recommend going back and reviewing the
material, especially chapters 13 and 14.
Move into part V when you're ready.

However, if you go no further in this book, please know
that you will have already gotten its primary gift.
If you now have a sense of the ego—what it is
and what it isn't . . .

If you have a sense of the matrix of delusion the ego spins . . .

If you have a sense of the problems this has gotten us into . . .

If you have a sense of the miracle of the multiverse
and your place in it . . .

If you have a sense of just how nonphysical reality is . . .

If you have a sense of how amazing human potential
and your unlimited nature are . . .

If you have a sense that there is an entirely new way to
be and live that is remarkably stress-free, fluid, fulfilling,
companionable, mutually supportive, and exciting and
you understand that this is your destiny and have a sense
of how to navigate your way to its shores, then . . .

Hooray!

I'm excited for you!

If you're not into spirituality and don't care so much
about enlightenment, you can skip the chapter text in this next
section. But do check out and do the practices!

If you're interested in how the ego co-opts religion
and spirituality, hiding the truth about everything
from being celibate to the way to manifest a Mercedes,
and if you're interested in a plainspoken discussion
about enlightenment . . . read on.

20

THE SPIRITUAL AND RELIGIOUS EGO

—

When you're spiritual, a mountain is not a mountain.
It's a pile of quantum quarks, or the repository of the
Akashic records, or Saint Germain's secret hideaway, or . . .
Stories all.

I f I had a dollar for every time I've heard somebody say, "I've got to get a handle on my ego," or said it myself, I'd have enough extra money to take a trip to Bali.

No one ever stops to wonder who the "I" is who is going to get a handle on his or her ego. And I never thought about it either. But when I did, it was like, "Oops."

Because the person who's going to get a handle on the ego is the spiritual ego—the "I" who's been meditating and reading all those self-help books—the religious ego I who's given all their wealth to the poor and prayed until their knees are bloody.

Yes. The ego is tricky.

It quite fancies the title "spiritual person" and "religious member" and has figured out that by *expanding* its identity to include religion and spirituality it can have its cake and eat it too.

The ego's whole gig is wanting to be more special. And what could possibly be more special than being spiritual?

Suddenly the "unspiritual me" that liked to drink vodka and get laid becomes the problem. The "old me" focused on material things; *that's* what was keeping happiness or self-realization or God at bay.

So I create a "new me" by educating the bad old me.

Maybe I search for enlightenment. Or maybe the old me dives into poverty and embraces chastity in order to switch hats and become more deserving of God's love.

Either way

I'm still little old ego me . . .

just in spiritual drag.

———

SPIRITUAL MATERIALISM AND THE current focus on manifesting wealth and abundance should be a dead giveaway that many New Age teachings reside at the lower end of the ego's needs hierarchy. But we don't see it because these teachings have been presented as "spiritual."

The endless wars and corruption, divisiveness and power brokering of world religions should be a dead giveaway that most religions and their followers are deeply mired in ego.

But we turn a blind eye because religion and spirituality hold a privileged position in our world. God is at the top of the totem pole. Kings and queens bowed to the church. The old habit of looking upward to God has translated into the habit of elevating anything that calls itself "spiritual" or religious as something special and above dispute.

Unless they've in some way embarrassed themselves beyond repair, clergy always rank at the top of the status heap as a breed apart. If we're told the person driving a clunker car shopping at the Salvation Army is spiritual, or that she's been meditating in an ashram for ten years, we get off the judgment wagon and nod respectfully.

Meditation can still trump a Mercedes.

People might think you're weird and invite you to dinner parties for your entertainment value. But there is still a certain deference conferred because your goals in life are obviously more elevated. And the ego, which is constantly concerned about other people's opinions and on the lookout for opportunities to gain self-esteem, is not likely to miss an advantage like that.

If we have little in the way of worldly goods, we can still stand in the grocery store line flipping through magazines we can't buy with food stamps looking at pictures of the British royals and the global elite and think, *It's easier for a camel to fit through the eye of a needle than it is for a rich man (or woman) to get into heaven* and feel quietly superior as we stick the magazine back on the shelf.

It's just what the ego does.

THE MORE THE EGO can clothe itself in accomplishments and glory, the better we feel about ourselves. Or at least that's the rationale. Thing is, we rarely feel better about ourselves no matter what we do, because:

Things and accomplishments don't shift the ego's perspective.

Priest, Nobel laureate, or Hollywood movie star, we still see ourselves as separate and alone just like our baby brains trained us to believe we are. Thus, until we start to move into transpersonal consciousness, we will *always* feel vulnerable and scared no matter how much stuff and glory we gather to us.

And *this* realization is what shifts us.

Viewed this way, it's a blessing the world is on such a materialistic binge. It's not until we buy and buy and have and have and do and do and strive and strive and discover that, "Dammit, I'm still me and I'm still scared and I'm still feeling disconnected," that we give up.

That's when we go, "Okay. What am I not seeing here?

"I have everything I could ever want and need. I've done all these things and learned all this stuff and proved myself over and over again. Why don't I love myself? Why am I still unhappy? Why isn't this working?"

That's when we begin to question the ego's perspective and values. That's when real change and a shift toward the transpersonal mind-set can occur.

But if we turn to religion to satisfy our deep need for wholeness and connection, if we become "spiritual" instead of diving into a thorough investigation of the nature of the ego and our real problem, the finish line gets pushed waaaaaay back.

We get sidetracked.

Suddenly we're immersed in astrology readings and prayer meetings and Bible school and crystal bowl chanting. We go to church or we attend spiritual retreats and study yoga. Either route, we get excited.

Thank God! There's a path out of the wilderness! There are things to do to mitigate our pain and confusion, our sense of disconnection from the world and other people. There's something meaningful about life after all!

Our gratitude is deep and sincere.

Very few of us are happy with who, what, and where we are, because in our ignorance about the ego, who we are seems so unsatisfactory and what we are is so limited and where we are is so uncomfortable.

We want to escape. We want to belong. We want to be better people living in better houses in a better world. We want to be special and deserving. We don't want to die. At the very least we want to feel good about ourselves while we're here on Earth.

And spirituality and religion promise much of this.

It's so much easier going the traditional route hanging out at church or the ashram with others than it is to do the solitary, painful work of putting our ego under the microscope! Yes, there are powerful spiritual systems such as Zen and Vipassana, A Course in Miracles, and Advaita—all of which are designed to expose and strip the ego away. But again, the ego is tricky.

Even formally pursuing stripping the ego away can become a practice that bolsters the ego. Plus, remember:

The ego loves complicated.

There are 19 major religions in the world, divided into some 270 major subdivisions. According to the *World Christian Encyclopedia*, Christianity alone has around 33,000 distinct denominations based on different beliefs and rules centered on varying scriptural interpretations and doctrine.

Pick one of these denominations and you can spend an entire lifetime navigating its unique philosophy. But let me ask you a question: Did Jesus come to start a religion for us to learn and study?

Did the Buddha?

Of course not.

As wonderful as many spiritual and religious systems are, as great as the camaraderie is, most cannot help but increase our dependency on looking outward for answers instead of searching inside ourselves like all the great teachers prompt us to do.

Only when it becomes obvious that one more seminar or Bible study class or book on Buddhism isn't going to do the job of getting us to I AM any more than one more job or raise or house is going to make us happy—only until it becomes obvious that the only path to I AM is a consistent, dedicated, quiet turning within that only we can do for ourselves does the quality and direction of our searching shift.

It took me seventeen years to get to that point.

It was 4 A.M.—my usual meditation start time—and instead of putting on music and lighting candles and incense, doing the breath work I'd learned, striving to move kundalini energy to my brain, doing a visualization technique, or om chanting while holding a mudra, I simply flopped down on my meditation pillow in exhaustion and said, "Fuck it."

I did!

I gave up.

I was so sick and tired of doing all the things I normally did for hours every day—even fiercely looking within—I couldn't do anything.

I simply closed my eyes and let it all go. And guess what?

I am

In an instant, that's all that was left!

Letting go of all systems and methods and trying was *the* tipping point on my spiritual journey. Everything changed from that morning onward. And yet it required thousands of dedicated hours of inner work and a lot of dabbling in systems for me to get to where I could let it all go so I AM could become apparent. After that nothing else mattered. I'd found the inner GPS that could guide me.

For you it will be different.

The journey to I AM and who you really are is *your* journey. It may take you five more minutes or five hundred more lifetimes. How it happens is uniquely your story. Wherever you find yourself on the path this moment is exactly perfect and where you are meant to be. All of it has brought you here, to this moment, reading these words:

Just as the finger pointing at the moon is

not the moon,

spiritual systems are not I AM.

This book is not I AM.

Systems and books are stories about I AM.

Do you want stories?

Or do you want

I AM

?

PRACTICE: SPIRITUAL DE-CLOAKING

Whether we're born into a religion or have stepped onto The Path later in life, stripping away the spiritual ego is not a fun project. Most of us have a lot of emotion invested in our spiritual identity—never mind time and money. It's the most predictable thing in the world for the ego to want to cling to the familiar ideas it has about God and to take comfort in knowing what it's supposed to be and how it's supposed to act within a particular system.

It takes an intrepid soul and a lot of determination to get beyond the stories the ego spins—especially the stories of religion and spirituality. But this can be done by mentally squaring our shoulders and gently asking ourselves some evocative questions.

Ready? Here goes:

If you turned to religion or spirituality for answers later in life, think back to that turning point. What were you looking for?

What did your heart and soul genuinely long for?

Have your spiritual pursuits since then given you what you want deep inside?

I remember when, about thirteen years into my spiritual quest for Truth, I hit a place of incredible self-satisfaction. Reincarnation? Soul retrieval? Enlightenment? How Creation started? Where we go after death? I had all the answers. All you needed to do was ask me. And if you didn't ask, I would volunteer what I'd learned anyway!

But where did I get the information?

I got it from books and teachers. Never mind that they all gave different answers to everything. Eventually I picked my favorite stories and stuck with them until they became *my* truth. And God help the person who tried to convince me of theirs!

And where was I AM in this whole process?

Nowhere I could access!

So think again about your initial leap onto The Path or into the pews. Who would you be if you had learned then what you're learning now?

Whether you made a transition into spirituality or were born into your current viewpoint, contemplate whether your beliefs are moving you toward I AM or away.

Do you often experience a profound sense of unification with the world and others? Are you happy for no reason? Is it hard to upset you? Are you moving beyond judgment and right and wrong, having discovered a more inclusive view? Congratulations!

Or have your beliefs caused problems? Distanced you from others? Has being a "spiritual person" made you feel superior?

Think about all the things you believe about what God is and how Creation works. Has your knowledge sprung from the deep, nonverbal waters of I AM within? Or has it been gleaned from outside sources?

If the latter, ask yourself: Can vast and subtle dimensions of Truth be poured into a cup that's already full? Can transformation occur within a static belief system?

This is a lot to contemplate. Don't be surprised if you feel resistance to the process. It's a basic human need to find answers in order to feel secure. And we've been programmed since kindergarten to obtain and trust answers from outside sources. Plus, it's a hell of a lot easier and quicker to pick up a book and read it on the subway on the way to work than it is to take the solitary time to go within. And OMG! What if what you find inside doesn't agree with what everybody else thinks?

Ding ding ding! Danger! Danger!

There's a reason most of us were raised not to mention religion or politics at the dinner table. But if we're going to get beyond the ego's grip, we have to understand the issues in which it's most invested.

Make sense?

So take a deep breath and dive on in. Don't worry. The water's fine.

21

LOOKING UP

—

S peaking of stories . . .

Ever driven in heavy traffic and stopped to let a driver cut in front of you and caught a subtle whisper: *There goes another tick in the* nice *column.* Or the flip side: You're driving in heavy traffic and somebody tries to cut in front and you speed up, closing the gap. *Oops. There goes another tick in the* naughty *column.*

Or you have a splitting headache and glance up, unconsciously thinking or saying, "Dear God, please take the pain away." Or maybe things go sideways on a project at work and you roll your eyes upward, muttering, "Heaven help us" to your business partner.

It's hard to get past the sense that someone overhead is watching, taking note of our goodness or badness. Almost everybody looks heavenward for reward or help when things get tough. It doesn't matter how many years we've been meditating or how many self-empowerment classes we've taken—most of us are still carrying around a subconscious divinity-in-the-sky program.

And it seems innocent. So you're looking up and asking for help, thinking and saying "God help me" or something similar. So what? Maybe you do it in jest. But this simple action is actually an enormous indicator of a deep, residual belief in separation between you and I AM.

And it doesn't matter if you change the wording from "God" to "Spirit" or "Consciousness" or "I AM" or the "Universe." If you're still looking to something *else*, separation is still a dominant part of your life.

The more aware I became of this subtle, ancient program, the more I caught myself doing it. I looked up a *lot*. And the gesture *always* carried with it a subtle plea for external, divine help.

It wasn't until I stopped doing this that I genuinely started entering into the power of I AM, letting it fill me in moments of confusion and pain instead of frittering away energy playing the game of separation and outside agency.

And, frankly, it scared the hell out of me.

The first few times I stopped myself from looking up, sincerely accepting that there isn't a damn thing *up there* that's going to rescue me or change me or do stuff for me, it freaked me out. I suddenly felt desperately alone and terribly anxious and abandoned. It was like, "Oh my God! Oh my God! I'm it? God help me!"

Ha! It took a few minutes each time to remember that it wasn't "me" left holding the bag and having to handle things; it wasn't me, Cate, who would deliver me from confusion, or bring the next job, or provide the healing for my pain or the world's pain.

It was I AM within me.

PRACTICE: STOP LOOKING UP

Watch yourself when you do something nice for someone. Notice if there's a slight inner sense of satisfaction knowing the big guy upstairs approves. Conversely, notice if you find yourself wincing over doing something "naughty."

Don't just shrug it off. Stop and *think* about it.

Why are you feeling guilty?

What story are you holding on to?

Who is keeping score?

Are you glancing skyward when you feel you need assistance? Do you find yourself saying things like "God help me" or "Heaven help us"? Are you waiting for the universe to guide you or "your spirit" to do such-and-such? When you catch yourself doing this, stop and energetically recenter your gaze "inward" instead of upward. Do a quick Stepping into Life exercise (pages 131–33).

Feel I AM within you.

Give thanks to I AM *within* you.

If you feel anxious and nervous or suddenly, overwhelmingly alone and scared, trust me, it's normal. Turning within and shouldering full responsibility for accepting I AM/God within is a *huge* deal. In those scary moments, make sure you practice the three steps of the embodying wholeness process: stopping, surrendering, and synthesizing.

Remember—it's not up to little old ego you.

22

EXTRA BAGGAGE

—

Spiritual matters are weighty matters.
Only religious matters are heavier.

I am

says it all, covers it all, includes all,

is all.

That's it.

Forget everything else, because

there is nothing else.

How simple can it get?

REMEMBER BACK IN CHAPTER 9 when I introduced you to I AM?

How long did that take?

Two minutes, max?

But the ego's ability to take something simple and turn it into a nightmare of complexity is supreme. Let's touch base with Sally Jane from Tallahassee for a moment and take a quick look at what the ego does with religion and spirituality.

After her breakdown from nervous exhaustion, Sally turns to God for answers.

Maybe she joins a church and hears some charismatic preacher cry: "Accept the Holy Spirit into your heart!"

She trembles and feels a deep yearning to do so. But being programmed into separation by her brain and society, she thinks the preacher means opening herself to something *outside* her. So she spends the next twenty years trying to become worthy of receiving the Holy Spirit, never realizing it's within her.

Or maybe she goes to a spiritual talk and a guru onstage points at her and roars: "You are God!"

How does she react?

She assumes they're referring to the only "I" she knows: her separate ego stuck somewhere in the first five levels of Maslow's needs hierarchy. "Me?" she says, startled and pleased, eyes wide, pointing a shaking finger at her chest. "Wow!"

But after the adrenaline rush is over and she's driving home with the environmentally friendly shopping bag filled with the teacher's videos and books and branded yoga pants on the seat beside her, she begins to wonder, *How do I live up to this?*

And the sad thing is, trapped in the ego matrix, she can't.

But she tries her best.

She gives up caffeine and meditates. She worries about her

carnal nature because deep down she has the feeling that sex, even with her husband, isn't spiritual. She squashes her emotions and tries to blank her mind. She wears white all the time because she identifies that with being pure until she reads all thirty-three books in the I AM series by Godfré Ray King and learns she should be wearing violet on Saturday and green on Wednesday and white only on Friday.

She strives and strives but somehow doesn't feel like she's getting anywhere.

Yes, she's happy doing what she's doing. She's discovered a profound purpose and has a supportive group of like-minded friends. And she's had a ton of insights into her (ultimately nonexistent) self and her issues.

But where is I AM in all this?

THE RELIGIOUS EGO IS all about conforming to enough rules (created by other egos) to get into heaven (which is already in us). The spiritual ego is usually about attaining enlightenment (which is the absence of ego altogether). Either way, Sally is trying to get through what's popularly called the "narrow gate to God" by *adding* to her existing persona. Which is why the gate to God is so narrow.[1]

Truth is, the gate is not narrow. It's that the ego gets ever wider.

PRACTICE: HI, ME!

This exercise is designed to stretch your boundaries and expand your awareness to consciously include other beings and more of life. I usually do this whenever I'm walking outdoors.

As you walk and notice things—the branches of a tree dripping with rain, a blossoming rhododendron, a great horned owl hooting in the forest, a crow calling overhead—greet them saying (or thinking), "Hi, me!"

Consciously acknowledge their individual presence while acknowledging the larger truth that these beings are not separate from you; that at the deepest level of what's real, they *are* you.

Just in a different form!

VARIATIONS:

Sometimes I'll see a horse galloping across a field or an eagle winging overhead and call out, "You're so beautiful!" Then, acknowledging union with that being, I immediately add, "I'm so beautiful!"

Or standing in awe of a sunrise or a view I say, "How stunning." And then I open my arms wide, taking the view into me, and say (or think) as I include myself in the picture: "I am so beautiful!"

Usually in that kind of glorious moment I say it out loud more than once. If no one's around, I *shout* it. Of course, if I'm at a backyard barbecue I just pause and drink in the beauty, then, in my mind's eye, step into the picture and include myself while thinking thoughts of gratitude and appreciation that include: "I am so beautiful!"

PEOPLE VARIATION:

I do the same thing when meeting people. This is trickier, because I'm usually so busy remembering names and responding to the person that I forget. But when they walk away I often watch them go thinking, "Hi, me. So nice to meet you and see myself in such a unique form doing such different work."

For a few moments I try to imagine that I'm walking away *as* that person. I put myself in their shoes for a few seconds.

This really helps drop barriers and judgment against people who think and believe differently than we do. They really are us, after all—just a different peak in the blanket with a different view!

23

THE LAW OF ATTRACTION

—

Wherever your nose is pointed,
that's where you're headed.

The Law of Attraction is probably *the* single-most popular system to be introduced into the spiritual arena ever. And the reason for this is . . . ?

Three guesses.

The Law of Attraction is not about transpersonal and transcendent mind. The Law of Attraction is not about spirituality. The Law of Attraction is about satisfying the needs and desires of the ego. And there's absolutely nothing wrong with this. As Maslow points out, we cannot attain greater consciousness until needs at lower levels have been satisfied to some extent. And just because physical needs lie at the base of the needs hierarchy doesn't make them "base."

So if you need a big house and a yacht to get past your self-esteem issues, if you believe you need a pile of money to feel secure, if you want to meet Mr. or Ms. Right so you can have the experience of feeling emotionally fulfilled . . . bring it on!

It's all part of life! It's all good!

The faster we get through these issues, the faster we get what we want, the faster we can move on . . . not that faster is any better than slower.

THERE'S NOTHING LIKE THE hope of ease and abundance to get the ego's attention. And who can blame anyone for seeking such things? I spent years working with the Law of Attraction before I refined the process and moved on. Working with the filmmakers of the movie *What the Bleep Do We Know!?* I was one of the people who helped it gain a foothold in the spiritual community in the first place.

Making a vision board and a list sure beats the hand some of us were given thirty-four hundred years ago:

> *Cursed is the ground for thy sake;*
> *in sorrow shalt thou eat of it all the days of thy life;*
> *Thorns also and thistles shall it bring forth to thee;*
> *and thou shalt eat the herb of the field;*
> *In the sweat of thy face shalt thou eat bread,*
> *till thou return unto the ground; for out of it wast*
> *thou taken: for dust thou art, and unto dust shalt thou return.*
> —GENESIS 3:17–19 KJV

Who in their right mind wants to sweat and toil for the rest of their lives if there's an easier option? Who doesn't long for gracious living, beauty, abundance, and good things: nice homes, cars and clothes, good food, vacations, and sexier smartphones?

It's all part of life and in our nature to desire.

So when somebody tells me quantum physicists are saying all

I have to do is "think and grow rich," what am I supposed to do? Say, "No, thank you. I like doing it the hard way"?

Of course not!

But as simple as the Law of Attraction is—and it doesn't get much simpler than "as you think and act so it is"—there is a *huge* problem with the formula. And the problem is this: the Law of Attraction as it is usually taught doesn't make it clear that it is I AM that does the manifesting, not "me" and the ego mind.

And as ego Cate, it's hard for me to get this.

After all, I'm the one doing the lists and the vision boards. I'm the one deciding what I want. And I'm told that once I place my mind on something I want and can visualize it clearly and focus on it, that that is what is affecting the quantum field, bringing me my reality.

And it is.

And a whole lot of other stuff as well.

EVER NOTICE WHAT HAPPENS when you go to manifest something? Sometimes you totally get what you want like magic. Sometimes you get pieces and parts. Often nothing happens at all. And most manifestations, when they do occur, seem to take forever.

Why is it such a hit-or-miss and lengthy affair?

The answer to that is a book in itself. But here's the short version: because the "I" that I think is doing the manifesting is the ego, and the ego is basically a schizophrenic dualistic illusory thought form.

And yet . . . the ego is also part of I AM.

That's where the ego gets its juice.

But the ego mind is fractured, noncohesive, and chaotic. It throws what little juice it has in a thousand different directions.

Yes, your thoughts affect the quantum field, and concentrated thought affects the quantum field more effectively. But for every sixty seconds of concentrated coherent thought you manage to give your dream of a new house, how many hours do you spend worrying about money and bills, the real estate market and your job, your relationship, whether the car needs an oil change, and and and . . . ?

Manifesting with the ego mind is like throwing a handful of pebbles into a quantum pond of water. Yes, your dream is one of those pebbles. And it's certainly one of the larger, heavier pebbles. But have you ever thrown a handful of pebbles into a pool of water?

Have you seen the amazing interference patterns created by all those stones hitting the water creating ripples? The same thing is happening with your thoughts in the quantum field. The ego mind is all over the place, constantly creating interference patterns that get in the way of manifestations.

As if all this weren't enough, here's another reason manifestation only works in a limited fashion: The ego is created out of the illusion of separation and is, therefore, ultimately itself an illusion.

Is it any wonder insecurity subconsciously pervades the human psyche? This is also why the ego can be such a jerk. It's obsessed with having things and looking good to make up for its awful powerlessness and subconscious fear of being exposed as the illusion it is. And fear and a subconscious belief in one's powerlessness do not make a great basis for manifesting.

SO LET'S GO BACK to Sally Jane again for a minute to see how all this plays out.

Sally and her husband bought into the refinancing craze,

figuring it would be a good idea to refinance their house with an adjustable-rate mortgage so they could finally get that college fund going. And then the housing bubble burst.

Now their payments are still rising, and Sally has no idea where the money's coming from to afford them. Tax laws are shifting against the middle class. Her daughter wants to take riding lessons, her car needs new tires, and she needs dental work, but her eighteen-hundred-dollars-a-month family insurance plan doesn't cover implants.

Day and night, her mind is filled with these kinds of very human concerns. But she's a spiritual person. She believes in the Law of Attraction. She owns copies of *The Secret* and *What the Bleep Do We Know!?* She listens to personal manifestation CDs on the way to work and knows that wealth and abundance are her genuine due if only she can make it happen.

But what is Sally going to put to work manifesting?

She thinks the mind that has to do the manifesting is *her* mind. It is, after all, the only mind she's ever known. So she cuts out pictures of piles of gold and jewels and other physical symbols of abundance that her *brain* associates with wealth and security and plasters them all over the house. She reminds herself of her abundance, chanting "I am abundant" whenever she remembers to do it.

After a year of chanting and adding more pictures to her screen-saver vision board and bathroom mirror, nothing has changed except inflation and the fact that now, in addition to all her other worries, Sally is convinced there's something wrong with her.

Other people are manifesting successfully.

"Did you hear?" a friend says over lunch. "Erica just manifested a trip to Maui! All expenses paid. Isn't that awesome?" Sally agrees it's awesome, finishes lunch, and pays, praying the charge will go through. She drives home on balding tires, feeling guilty and depressed.

Why can't she get it right like Erica?

TRUTH IS SUPPOSED TO set us free, not bury us deeper in a hole.

Unfortunately, Sally is far more likely to blame herself for not being able to manifest than she is to question the value system that set this goal as important for her to accomplish in the first place. Nor will she question the manifestation formula she picked up somewhere. She'll probably use the last bit on her credit card to pay for another seminar, because she's been taught "to be abundant, you have to think abundant. And if you have to fake it till you make it, fake it."

But what mind is at work here?

Sally is at the end of her rope because she's locked into an ego mind-set and its identity as a limited physical human—which can't manifest diddly squat.

She's lost in the vanity and pressure of thinking she can do it.

She's bought into the lie that *she* is powerful.

Abundance is the ground of her being, creation the very core of her nature. But she totally ignores the consciousness supporting her, available to effortlessly extend support to her dreams.

How can she possibly miss this?

She misses the abundant nature of I AM—the reality underpinning her life—the same way it's possible to miss a gorilla in a hallway. Sally has narrowed her focus onto the explicate order: externals. She's counting balls.

• She isn't seeking *within* for the implicate order I AM.

- She's obsessed with things that she (naturally) perceives are outside of her, like money and mortgages and trips to Maui.
- She isn't seeking an expanded view or a greater mind.
- She isn't dropping layers of identity and getting out of the ego matrix.
- She isn't leaning on I AM in deep trust and joy, knowing her every need is fulfilled before she can even ask.

Sally is looking for an easy way out of her money problems and unhappiness.

She's gilding the ego cage that keeps her prisoner.

THE LATIN ROOT OF the word "manipulation" is *manus*, meaning "hand." Which is the same root for the words "manifest" and "manifestation."

As we think and act, so we become.

But what are we thinking? How are we acting? What are we becoming?

Instead of dissolving the illusions of the personal self, instead of desiring to consciously dissolve into I AM so we can enjoy the natural abundance of our true nature, we're trying to manipulate the quantum field to attract what we desire. And whether it's gold or a convertible or a mate, this process is all about outside agency and separation.

I am one thing, the object of my desire is another thing, and the quantum field is yet a third thing to be affected by "my" (fourth thing) ego thoughts.

It's also about feeling good about ourselves and what I EGO can do.

Indeed, the Sanskrit word used to describe such human powers as personal manifestation is *siddhi,* which means accomplishment and success. And in India, the truly advanced students shun those who teach how to gain these powers, shaking their heads in dismay over the trap they unknowingly set.

"The path of seeking *siddhis* is dangerous," an Indian doctor from Tamil Nadu said to me one day as we were talking about all this. "People can lose themselves down that path for thousands of incarnations. You're lucky you escaped."

———

THE KEY TO MANIFESTATION is surrendering our sense of separation—the linchpin illusion of the ego—and wallowing in the delicious knowledge that:

I am

all things.

Everything I desire

is already part of me.

Remember: the book of Matthew doesn't say, seek ye things and the kingdom of God will be yours. It says: *Seek ye first the kingdom of God . . . and all these things shall be added unto you.* And the kingdom of God is the consciousness.

I am.

That's the key.

PRACTICE: MANIFESTING FROM SOURCE

The best way I know to manifest is to forget about manifesting.

Really.

Manifesting is I AM's job, not the splintered-off portion you call "yourself."

The whole blanket is what's going to gather its forces to bring things your way, not the peak in the blanket called "Heather" or "Harry." And grasping this distinction and leaning on the whole blanket and giving credit where credit is due are the most important parts of the manifestation process.

As (apparently) individual human beings our job is to 1) understand the ego and do the work necessary to embody I AM, 2) know what we want, 3) do the physical work needed to align ourselves with our dreams and make our dreams happen, 4) get out of the way, and 5) prepare ourselves to receive.

It's kind of a ten-step, five-Gs formula:

Get aware:
1) Use the practices detailed in this book to become aware of I AM consciousness.
2) Know that you, I AM, and your dream are *one* thing.

Get clear on your ego needs:
3) Decide what you want.
4) Realistically assess your dream or desire.

Get going:
5) Choose the actions that feel right that will take you physically in the direction of your dream.
6) Take those actions and stick to them.

Get out of your head:

7) Be undaunted that it's a million-mile journey.

8) Have no expectations about what your manifestation will look like or how it will show up. Know I AM is aligning things so you will have what you want.

Get ready:

9) Open up to receive the opportunities and inner promptings taking you to your dream.

10) Feel the reality of your dream in your life and be *grateful.*

Ignore the voices in your head saying you can't do it or that you're on the wrong path. 1) It's not "you" that is responsible for the manifestation in the first place (what a relief!) and 2) there is no wrong path. If you're on it, it's the right path. And if you find yourself someplace you don't want to be, take another path.

Learn to ignore the insanity of the ego mind as it tries to sabotage things by telling you you're not worthy of having what you want . . . how your mother did this or your father didn't do that or how you don't have a college degree . . . all the conditions and reasons for failure the ego loves to dwell on. Remember all of that is just voices in your head.

I AM/LIFE knows the right timing for manifestations better than your ego. I AM/LIFE knows all the things that need to happen and line up to facilitate a manifestation; your ego doesn't. Simply declare what you want. Take steps to make it happen. Be open. Don't stress. Be happy and grateful and let it go.

General happiness for no reason is a *huge* indicator that you are embodying the truth that you are I AM/LIFE. If you're happy and fulfilled *without* a particular dream and your happiness isn't based on something manifesting, that attitude helps pave the way.

*If you're genuinely already happy . . .
what more do you need?*

MORE DETAILS:

If you want to make a list, make a list.

Lists create clarity. How can I AM do its thing if you are not clear? (And you are I AM!) After I make a list for clarity, I throw it away.

ACTION:

A lot of people seem to think manifestation means making a list then folding their hands and waiting for things to fall into their lap. Not so.

Manifestation is a holistic practice, which means putting your head and heart in the game, your hand on the tiller of life, and doing the work of aligning your physical circumstances and your mental and emotional life with your dream.

No matter your situation, put your feet on the physical path of becoming and having what you want and don't leave it for anything. Do what it takes. Which brings us to another vital piece of the manifestation process.

PASSION:

Emotion is *far* more powerful than the mind when it comes to manifesting. The electromagnetic field of the heart is sixty times greater than the brain.[1] And when I'm in a loving, unified, heart-felt space, the harmonious energy field of my heart can entrain other people's brain waves several feet away without me even touching them.[2]

One of the biggest stumbling blocks to manifestation for people is lack of emotional juice. Powerful desire is a force to be reckoned with. Powerful desire can drive a human being into the fifth level of self-actualization. It's no coincidence the root words "act" and "actual" are part of the description for that needs level.

If you're lazing along in life, sort of confused, not rocking the boat, generally feeling like you haven't gotten the things you deserve and want—you're most likely approaching manifestation the same way you live.

If you're not jazzed by anything and not certain what you want to do or where you want to go or how you want to be and you're using the manifestation of *stuff* to fill in the blanks of your life, you're not coming from passion and growth.

You're coming from boredom and lack. What to do?

If you find yourself in this position:

Get passionate about

wanting to be passionate about something!

Make passion the first thing you manifest! (For more detail, go back to the exercise in chapter 4.)

BE GRATEFUL:

Ever notice how quickly the ego moves from one desire to the next? You want a new car and get a new car, and once you get it you already want a boat to go behind the car. Or a bigger flat-screen TV for the family room.

I watched this in action while writing this book.

I was staying at a friend's house on the island of Paros in Greece and took a break to go for a walk. The pebbles on the beach below the house were gorgeous. (The island has been a marble quarry site since antiquity.) And I noticed how I would see one glowing pebble, pounce on it, pick it up, and even before I looked at what I had in my hand my eyes were already roving the beach for the next pebble.

That's the insatiable ego for you.

It's rarely grateful and it never has enough.

So grease the wheels of manifestation by being genuinely grateful for life and everything you have *now*. Give thanks for the pebbles in hand.

24

THE HIGHER SELF

—

*Higher versus lower is just a concept
our brains give us.*

Here's another confusing story the ego has perpetuated.

Spiritual people (myself included once upon a time) are constantly talking about their Higher Self and their lower self—also frequently referred to as their "God Self" and their lower "human self."

So what is this God Self—the greater self, the real self, the Higher Self, the "God of my being" that so many millions desire and search for and hope will appear to supply their needs someday?

This is a trick question.

There is no Higher Self because there is no personal self to begin with—lesser or otherwise. There is only one "thing" in all of existence: I AM.

Remember the blanket.

Remember that despite all the talk about the needs hierarchy and the ego's evolution, the ego is actually a total *illusion* based in the lie of separation my brain tells me is real as a baby. It's a bunch of words in my head. And as the contents in my head change and evolve, it seems "I" am changing.

> *But as long as there is any sense of*
> *personal identity,*
> *all that's changing is the illusion.*

The whole thing about higher and lower selves is the ego performing doublespeak in the story of life, ensuring the survival of its illusion of existence by proclaiming itself a "lower self" on the hunt for something greater than itself—thus solidifying its existence by the fact of its search.

You've got to hand it to the ego. For an illusion it's wicked clever.

And while we're living in this world of appearances, it's a freaking circus act trying to make sense of all this because "this world" isn't real the way we think real is at all. And the words used to explain this unreal world of appearances don't describe reality.

Concepts like "higher" and "lower" selves are conveniences that help us navigate this odd reality. I couldn't talk about any of this stuff without using words like "I AM" and "ego" and "self" and "myself" and "you" and "I" and "us" and "we."

But all of it is pure story . . . except, of course

> *I am*

PRACTICE: DEALING WITH PROBLEMS

Remember the Stepping into Life process (pages 131–33)? I did it a *lot* as a way to expand my identity to include the vastness of the world beyond "me." It's great for dropping the illusion of boundaries. And I still do it all the time.

But there's also a way of using this process to put problems in perspective.

First off: Ask yourself, "What are my problems?"

Make a list and write down your problems: e.g., I'm overweight. I don't have enough money. My kid is on drugs. I don't like my job. My spouse is having an affair. . . . Whatever your problems are, write them down.

As you're writing, notice any feelings and emotions that are evoked. Is doing this list making you anxious? Do you feel any sensations in your body?

Really tune in and notice how thinking about all your problems makes you feel.

Now, go find a quiet space and sit down—preferably outdoors, and definitely someplace you won't be disturbed by phones and other people's noise and demands.

Relax and breathe calmly for a couple of minutes.

Do the Stepping into Life process.

At the end of the process when you are immersed in the vision of the whole world as part of you, slowly say (or think) the following:

I am all life.

I am one with all I see.

I am one with all I don't see.

This is my supply.

This is my support.

All life is supporting me.

I am

Look around with normal vision.
See how *vast* this world is!
Realize how enormously filled with energy it is.
The sky, the earth, the trees and plants and animals and wind and buildings and people are part of you. While looking around with normal vision acknowledge:

This is my supply.

All of this is me.

This is what

I am

With this truth in mind, think of one problem.
Again, slowly look around, paying attention, absorbing the world, and think or say:

This is my supply

All of this is one with me

This is what

I am

Feel the *hugeness* of what you are. Sense the true nature of your being and the enormity of your supply.
How does "your" problem look now?

THE STEPPING INTO LIFE process isn't going to solve the problem of a friend or loved one with cancer. *What it does do is give you a much broader perspective.*

With all life as you, with all life as your unlimited resource—your problems take on a different hue and texture. Doing this process loosens a problem's hold on you and enables you to loosen your grip on it.

Seething and worrying over something, our whole reality restricts. And the more restricted we become, the larger our problems loom.

They become our world. And who wants their problems as their whole reality?

Play with this.

Pick one problem at a time. Do the Stepping into Life process and then practice moving back and forth between the state of Oneness with the world around you and the worry-state of your constricted ego focused on a problem.

Sense the difference in the energy and how you feel in both states.

Remember: The larger your consciousness, the greater the resources, energies, and opportunities you draw to you to assist with problems.

THE IMITATION GAME

Trying to be other than I am
because I judge what I am
is hell.

The ego knows *about* enlightenment. But it doesn't know enlightenment. It knows what it perceives about the qualities of enlightenment that awakened beings demonstrate—qualities such as detachment, desirelessness, and selflessness. But the ego has none of these qualities itself. Which is why it has a hard time understanding them.

But it has *ideas* about them.

Like a monkey mimicking a man, the ego watches or reads about what an awake being does and then tries to copy the *external* actions it sees. Take selflessness as an example.

Enlightened beings cannot fail being selfless because they have no sense of a separate self. That *is* the state of enlightenment. They cannot fail but to act for the best of the whole because they consciously *are* the whole. It could thus be said that the enlightened being is actually quite selfish, always acting on their own behalf, because they are one with life itself.

But interpreting the actions of the selfless being the ego thinks, "I must not be selfish. I must put others before me. I should always consider others first."

The ego hasn't a clue that not being selfish is not selflessness. And even though it's *miserable* constantly denying its own needs in favor of others'—and we're not very pleasant to be around as a result of our self-denial—the ego reward gained is the profound satisfaction of knowing we're living up to the spiritual rule that says "Thou shalt not be selfish."

Plus, we get a bonus.

Misery too is a sign of advanced spirituality. Haven't we been taught how noble it is to suffer like Jesus did?

We must be gaining ground!

———

DESIRELESSNESS IS ANOTHER NATURAL characteristic of the awakened mind. But for ego me to accomplish a facsimile I have to twist desirelessness into the pretense of not wanting things. I have to pretend I don't want cars and money and love and sex and relationships and all the other things I've been told aren't spiritual.

I have to *act* like I'm detached and have no desires.

But desire is responsible for everything from our hairdos to the cars we drive. Desire brings children into the world. Desire for enlightenment puts people on The Path. Desire created French cuisine and drove Madame Curie to discover radiation and Einstein to discover relativity. Desire is responsible for everything beautiful in the world, not just pain and suffering when personal ego expectations and individual hopes are dashed.

Trying to destroy desire in a human being still operating within the illusion of personal identity is bound to destroy the person attempting this strange feat. And the disastrous effect of this unnatural act on the surrounding people and environment is equally unfortunate.

Sexual abuse by "celibate" priests affects more than 95 percent of church dioceses and approximately 60 percent of all religious communities[1]—and these figures are low, because many cases of abuse are still never reported. So far the Vatican has paid out more than $3 billion to American dioceses to cover the costs of sex-abuse scandals.[2]

And how about that poverty rule?

An enlightened being doesn't need to own anything because they already *are* everything. The enlightened being has nothing to prove and recognizes the perfection of everything, just as it is. For such a consciousness, living in a penthouse or a flophouse is inconsequential.

Which doesn't mean there aren't preferences.

Even chipmunks prefer being warm, dry, and fed rather than cold, wet, and hungry. And enlightenment doesn't mean we can't own things or live in a penthouse. We can freely do any damn thing we choose. It's just that the *importance* of these things has evaporated.

Attached to nothing and no one, with no need to be a certain way or have certain things, not attached to issues or hang-ups, a state of great fluidity is theirs. The enlightened being isn't spiritual in the slightest.

The enlightened being is free.

―――――

THE EGO, ON THE other hand, is not free. Especially burdened as it is with all its concerns about looking good and following the rules.

Worse, trying to do stuff because we think it's spiritual just takes us deeper into the ego and farther away from I AM.

I remember what happened when my first teacher told me I had to give up meat if I wanted to "attain." I gave it up. I believed in a vegetarian diet, but I still *wanted* meat, especially bacon and fried chicken.

And I denied what I wanted.

What did this accomplish?

It set in motion a part of me that wanted one thing and another part of me that wanted another thing, and then a dynamic was created pitting these two parts against each other.

Not only did this multiply the voices in my head, it firmly rooted me in the dualistic mind-set that judges one thing as good and its opposite as bad. Also, it set up a pattern of self-judgment where my self-esteem now depended on whether I managed to stick to my vegetarian ideals or succumbed to the spiced meatballs at the office Christmas party.

A formula for enlightenment?

How about a formula for guilt?

I want a BLT, but instead I buy hickory-smoked tempeh to go with my lettuce and tomato sandwich. Internal pressure and frustrated desire build. My life starts to change in ways that reflect my growing issues around food.

I stop going to my favorite grocery store because the scent of fried chicken in the deli torments me. I start avoiding certain people because they eat meat. I start making them wrong. I overeat carbs for satisfaction and gain weight.

Now I hate my body whenever I look in the mirror.

To bolster my self-esteem and further justify my choices, I read all the literature about how great for the planet not eating meat is. I decide to go vegan and take a vegan cooking class. I join a vegan food-buyers club, get all excited, and start a *Vegans for the Environment* newsletter. Soon I'm searching for advertisers so I can make the newsletter a full-time job aligned with my values.

Wonderful! But how much closer to I AM have I gotten?

Vegetarianism works great for a lot of people. Cutting back on meat consumption is scientifically proven to be healthier for the planet and our bodies, not to mention it removes the need to kill animals. And yes, if humans ate less meat and raised fewer cows, methane levels would drop and we'd mitigate climate change while helping save the rain forests.

But for myself?

All I've done is spin a more complex story within the ego matrix, miss out on things I enjoy, rag on myself, and create unnecessary misery.

Enlightenment cannot be manufactured or imitated, accomplished or attained. As Isha Yoga founder Sadhguru Jaggi Vasudev puts it, "If you allow life to happen to you in its utmost possibility, enlightenment is a natural flowering."

In the meantime I'm eating bacon.

PRACTICE: WHERE AM I NOT REAL?

Desire is a very real indicator that something remains incomplete. We cannot transcend or evolve beyond what we have not yet experienced and embraced.

With this in mind, take stock of your life:

- Are there things you're not doing because you think they're not spiritual?
- Are there things you desire that you pretend not to want?
- Are there things you're doing only because you think you "should" be doing them?

Be honest with yourself and write them down.

Now, imagine not doing the things you don't want to do, and doing and having what you really desire. What would that be like? Who would you be? Where would you be? What would you be doing?

Imagine this and feel how it feels.

Congratulations.

You now have a great list of things to surrender to I AM for manifesting!

THE REAL DEAL

—

Maybe the word "enlightenment" should be changed to "endeadenment"?
Somehow I just can't see a lot of eager seekers signing up
for a weekend seminar on "How to Become Endeadened."

For thousands of years we've been given things to do and words to chant, sacred books to read and clothes to wear, special foods to eat and certain things to think and say in order to become enlightened.

Which would seem to imply a "me" that can be enlightened. Right?

When Buddha says, "I am awake," and Jesus says, "I and my Father are one," from the ego perspective what else can we assume other than the existence of an "I" capable of waking up and becoming one with God?

And herein lies the whole problem with spirituality: There are two interpretations of the word "I."

And even though one of these perspectives
is an illusion,

both are taken as real.

———

MOST PEOPLE ARE ONLY aware of the body-based I EGO perspective. Even if the ego perspective is dropped for brief periods during meditation or through the use of plant medicines, the ego almost always ends up back in the driver's seat, busily co-opting Truth and reshaping it into the illusion of "me" having "had" an experience of Oneness that I then go out and talk about.

I did it until I realized what I was doing. And I frequently find myself in the unpleasant situation of being in discussions with other people who make the same mistake. "I've had plenty of enlightenment experiences," a man recently declared at a dinner party. "I know the Truth."

But if he really knew the Truth, he wouldn't have laid claim to it. If enlightenment had occurred, even momentarily, he should have admitted he *couldn't* lay claim to it because enlightenment is the end of the personal perspective. It's the *death* of the ego. Game over.

Kaput. *Finito.*

But because almost nobody understands this, most people think, "Yeah. Death of the ego. Cool. I want that."

They have no idea what they're saying.

According to Sadhguru, my teacher from Tamil Nadu (and the last teacher I'll ever have aside from I AM), awakened beings usually have difficulty staying in the body after enlightenment occurs. He personally has devised a way to retain his body through an alchemical anchor he's created—a copper ankle bracelet with a piece of string binding his energies to the bodies of three brahmacharis currently living. They keep him anchored so he can complete his work until the date he's foreseen arrives, whereupon he will sever the tie and go.

He also talks about his wife, Vijaykumari, and how she finished the dishes after lunch one day, took off her metal jewelry (metal binds consciousness energetically), sat down in meditation, and left her body. The grave where her body is buried is now a lovely spot on the grounds of Sadhguru's ashram in Cooimbatore.

Apparently awakening and death of the body is far more common than awakening and sticking around. The consciousness is so unfettered when the ego dissolves that the body can't hold the energies and the consciousness leaves—a fact that's shocked some of my spiritual friends when I've told them.

"Why haven't I heard about this?" people ask.

At which I shrug and say, "I don't know. But it sure is lousy news to spread if you're in the enlightenment business."

THIS IS WHY 99 percent of all spiritual people in the world should get over wanting enlightenment. It's absolutely, positively *not* what they're looking for.

Humans want information about what will make life better—not effectively end it. They want to know how to stop being unhappy with themselves or their spouse or more successful at making money. And this is what most Western spiritual "gurus" teach.

Awakened teachers (if you can find one) rarely bother trying to explain enlightenment because they know it's not what most people really want. Plus they know it's impossible to explain and almost nobody will wake up no matter what they say anyway. They also know whatever they do say will be misunderstood and most likely turned into some sort of dogma by people's egos.

So why bother?

Frankly I have no idea why enlightenment is being sold to people as the greatest thing since sliced bread and the answer to all pain and suffering and the end of every cash-flow problem.

Of course enlightenment actually *is* the greatest thing since sliced bread as well as the answer to all pain and suffering and the end of every cash-flow problem.

Just not in the way people think.

Bottom line, there is no one left standing at the end to have become enlightened.

It really is

the end.

PRACTICE: REDEFINING SUCCESS

The ego is all about success and through material and spiritual accomplishments proving how wonderful it is. I AM is all about life and living and learning.

Life itself often helps us discover the difference in later years. We call it midlife crisis and second childhood—periods where we suddenly realize we are halfway to the finish line or more and suddenly it's like "WTF have I been doing with my life?" and we start reassessing everything in terms of personal fulfillment instead of social appearances.

But why wait until midlife?

In the land of the blind, the one-eyed man is king.

If we spend time and effort early in life learning who we really are, what's real, how life works, how the ego works, and how consciousness works, we're far ahead of those who are blindly focused on the same old things that have gotten us into the scary pickle we find ourselves in today.

If you know how life works success is guaranteed because at that point *you* are in charge and the one defining success. The only question is: How do I learn to perceive things the way they really are? And if you've come this far you already know the answer:

1) Learn to understand the nature of the ego mind and cultivate a transpersonal view of life by spending an hour a day in self-reflection and meditation.
2) Surrender to I AM.

It's also not a bad idea to take the following old Zen saying to heart:

You should sit in nature for twenty minutes a day unless you're busy. If you're busy, you should sit for an hour.

Get your kids out in nature as much as possible. Studies of children with ADD and ADHD indicate that the more kids get out into green spaces, woods, and parks and play, the calmer they get. Some have reduced or even gotten off their medications this way.[1]

And yes, I know I sound like a broken record, but turn off the phone, unplug, and get acquainted with silence. When you jog, run to the sound of your breath and footfalls. Tune *into* your body and inner being, not away.

You don't have to be weird about it. But the less stimulation and noise in your head, the more capable you will be of hearing the still, small voice of I AM within . . . the greatest guide and lover and power source ever.

These are simple things to do that have profound results. And yet they are the hardest things for the ego to do because:

1) None of these things are glamorous.
2) They take time and mindfulness.
3) They work.

These things are lifestyle changes that require nothing less than *a willingness to reprioritize and change how you live.* And the ego doesn't want that. How much more pleasurable for the ego to keep the status quo! How much more impressive it is to go on a cleanse or take an expensive Ayurvedic yoga retreat in Bali!

So if you're experiencing resistance to doing the simple, unglamorous things that are recommended in this book . . . now you know why.

27

BUDDHA NATURE

—

Buddha nature?
It's a fact . . .

What conversation about enlightenment is complete without an obscure, confusing Zen-like conversation about Buddha nature?

So here goes!

According to Zen legend, when the Buddha awakened, he said, "Isn't it remarkable! All beings are already enlightened!"

And he's right.

In the enlightened state everyone is enlightened

because everything is One thing.

When I'm awake everyone is awake

because they are all me

(even though there is no "me").

Bottom line:

I AM is not fooled by the illusion that there are others, let alone the story that others are asleep.

The "already enlightened" state is referred to as the Buddha nature— which is the truth that all is One.

Not the realization that all is One, but the fact of it.

All is One.

I STRESS THE FACT of Oneness instead of its realization because the word "realization" means there's something that needs to be realized, which is patently not true if everybody is already enlightened. Realization also implies there is someone who can "do" the realizing, which is no more possible than "me" getting enlightened.

So the very concept of "realizing the Buddha nature" is a falsehood—a half-truth that sounds incredibly true, another ego interpretation, this time of something the Buddha said, that is totally misleading. It also, of course, "coincidentally" supports the idea that the ego can realize enlightenment.

Nitpicky?

Not if you want to get your nonexistent head around the Truth.

Unfortunately, the *fact* that everybody is already enlightened is only obvious if you're not in the ego dream of separation. Once outside the illusion it's perfectly obvious that the Buddha nature cannot and does not belong to anyone.

There is no *my* Buddha nature. No one *has* a Buddha nature, just as there is no *my* Higher Self or *my* God. There is no "me" to begin with to "have" anything.

But inside the dream, the *fact* of Oneness (Buddha nature) suddenly becomes a quality to possess—a goal to acquire. The ego comes along and does its thing, creating an interpretation that can't help but be half-assed because the ego and the separate self *is* the illusion and can't possibly understand what it's not (real) let alone speak truth about reality, which is:

The fact of Buddha nature.

PRACTICE: DISCERNMENT

There's no way to practice Buddha nature. But it takes discernment to know that. It takes discernment to be able to see through the fabric of lies and nice-sounding half-truths the ego tells us about ourselves, the world, spirituality, and everything else.

It's not that the ego is a liar. It's just that the ego has no grasp of Truth. And what is Truth?

I am

Pure and simple

The point of this book is not helping people achieve a state of zombielike mindlessness or the impossible goal of achieving enlightenment and Buddha nature. It's about recognizing the ego so we can escape our mindless identification with it that keeps us

> *but a walking shadow, a poor player*
> *that struts and frets his hour upon the stage . . .*
> *full of sound and fury, signifying nothing.*
> —*MACBETH*, ACT 5, SCENE 5

To develop discernment, contemplate I AM. Contemplate the ego. How it is created. How it functions. Do the exercises in this book.

Contemplate what's "real." Use your beautiful mind to play with ideas you've never thought about before. Forget your problems for an hour every day. Look up at the night sky and pick a star and imagine its consciousness. Fill yourself with the intoxication of I AM. Ask for a new mind! For brilliance!

And see what these new thoughts and desires bring.

28

THE GRAND DESIGN

—

Life is all there is.
And once beyond the ego's mad illusions it's all it ever should
be . . . and then more. Always more.

There is such a thing as Truth with a capital T. A place of absolutes and absolution. A state of mind where it all comes clear.

Growing up in the insanity of a dysfunctional family in this desperately dysfunctional world, as a child I longed for nothing more than sanity. I actually fantasized that the *Enterprise* would trip through time and Mr. Spock would land a shuttle down by the farm pond below the horse barn and sit and talk with me. At the end of our conversations he always gave me the choice to stay here on Earth or go with him to explore the stars.

And because I longed for peace and equanimity, because there was something inside me that said there must be a place where the search for what is real and true in ourselves is supported and allowed to unfold unmolested, and because such a place apparently didn't exist yet on my planet—I always chose to go.

If somebody had told the fantasy-prone, emotionally bruised thirteen-year-old girl lying in bed listening to her alcoholic stepfather abuse her gentle, peace-loving mother; if somebody had told the desperately unhappy twenty-nine-year-old divorcée addicted to alcohol, cigarettes, and pain that it would take until she was sixty to find lasting peace and, better than that, *answers* to life's major questions . . . all I can say is thank God no one did, for I know exactly what I would have thought if they had:

Sixty? Please. Somebody shoot me now.

But times have changed. When I was thirteen and twenty-nine, there were no books like this in the stores and the local library. No Internet where a simple Google search revealed the wisdom of the ages. No hint of the existence of an overarching absolving Truth that makes genuine sense of the madness of the world.

There was simply the madness of the world—tons of churches and politicians and advertisers and activists waving their special brand of truth like a banner, telling me to believe this, that, and the other thing, trying—loudly—to convince anyone who would listen that theirs was the only rock of salvation.

When I got on the spiritual path, I was greeted by people who loved to talk in more egalitarian terms about "their" truth and "my" truth and "your" truth and everybody's "individual truth." And I bought into the alphabet-soup approach to truth for a while because it was so gently offered.

But holy ego-speak Batman!

There is no such thing as individual truth, because, for starters, the whole "individual" thing is ultimately an illusion. It's all blanket. Remember? But the ego loves to twist things so it looks good. And it has taken the words "opinion" and "belief" and spit polished them into the spiritual notion of individual truth (which sounds ever so much nicer). There's so much insistence about it, so much misunderstanding, that talking about *the* Truth seems somehow politically incorrect.

Like, "How *dare* you presume?"

Which is where Rhiannon was coming from when she bit my head off at Thanksgiving dinner that day. She'd never gone deep enough within the cave of her own being to get beyond the yammering of ego voices in her head. She'd never experienced the place of union where all the conflicting opinions and beliefs and stories of the mind are wiped away.

She couldn't imagine a place that was free of personal agenda.

No wonder she attacked!

All she heard that day was one more ego voice—in this case mine—waving a flag declaring I had the Truth. And she looked at my individual life with all its typical human issues—my frustration about a lack of money and success, my opinionated brashness— and went, "Nope. No way can I accept that this person knows *the* Truth."

And she was right.

That person *didn't* know the Truth.

"I" still don't.

For "me" to "know the truth" is to stand outside of it. And the Truth is:

I am the Truth.

And so are you.

————

THERE IS SUCH A thing as Truth with a capital T. And the only place it can be found is within you.

Which maybe sounds lonely . . . but it's not. Because all of existence lies within. All life. It's right inside. And when you realize this, when you step beyond the personal into the transpersonal and transcendent states of mind where complete understanding of self and life and the human condition and our evolutionary journey is found, the Truth washes away the confusion and fear, conflict and doubt, and you are free.

Free to be and do and live and love and create however you desire.

At the end of the path of seeking lies peace so effortless and abiding that you wake in the morning with a smile on your lips and you leap up to greet the day with gladness and passion. For at the end of the path of seeking you have discovered that the real purpose of life is:

Life Itself

You have discovered that:

I am . . . just is.

And I am human is I am's story.

We aren't souls on the frontiers of existence.

We are the frontier.

Bon voyage.

ACKNOWLEDGMENTS

—

I t takes a village to raise a child, and a book is not much different. First and foremost (and given the material it would be accurate to say "only"), I would like to thank I AM for picking me up like a rag doll in December 2014 and relentlessly shaking me until all the words were on the page. I truly had no choice in the matter. After that the miracle of multiplicity in Oneness took over—which means there are a lot of people I'd like to thank for making *The E-Word* possible.

While bringing this book to print, my agent, Lisa Hagan, has become a dear friend. The quintessential agent every writer dreams of—kick-ass businesswoman, fierce mama bear, advocate, encouraging companion, "commiserator" (there should be such a word), and coach. Lisa, I'm *so* blessed to have you on this writing journey with me!

Thank you to Zhena Muzyka, my publisher and editor. What can I say? Z went out on a limb for this book and guided its development with a loving yet firm hand every inch of the way. She was spot-on with every editorial comment, had a vision for how to present it to the world, and has done everything in her power to bring that vision to light. Bless you and thank you!

To Jesse, my friend and most loyal reader. God knows how many editions I subjected you to. But you read them and made all the right approval noises writers look for each time. Thank you!

And Pat—wow. Thanks for opening the doors of your house on Paros, ensuring stable Internet access on a remote spot on an island at considerable cost and effort, leaving me totally alone to write and brood and walk and sleep and go through all the emotional peaks and valleys writers go through while never once asking me to cook. The graciousness of your hospitality and the beauty of Paros are embedded in every page.

To all my friends who endured months of absence, canceled dinners, and God knows what else because "I'm writing": Thanks for still being there when I came back from the abyss.

Thanks to Shelley, my designer, who created all the graphics and the great cartoon. Thanks to Faren Bachelis, meticulous copy editor; Haley Weaver, editorial assistant; and all the designers and production staff at Enliven—what a help you've been, and what a beautiful job you've done making the physical book exciting to look at, hold, and read.

Last, but far from least, I'd like to thank every single person who reads this book. The baton I AM handed me expands outward with you.

NOTES

CHAPTER 4: AFTERWARD

1. Richard Bach, *Illusions: The Adventures of a Reluctant Messiah* (New York: Delta, 1998).

CHAPTER 5: NO JOY IN MUDVILLE

1. Lilly Wachowski and Lana Wachowski, *The Matrix*, Warner Bros., 1999.
2. World Food Programme, "And the Nominees Are . . . Helping Hungry People Around the World, Says WFP," January 24, 2007, www.wfp.org/news/news-release/and-nominees-are -helping-hungry-people-around-world-says-wfp.
3. Centers for Disease Control and Prevention, *Public Health Action Plan to Integrate Mental Health Promotion and Mental Illness Prevention with Chronic Disease Prevention, 2011–2015* (Atlanta: US Department of Health and Human Services, 2011).
4. Wachowski and Wachowski, *The Matrix*.
5. Lori M. Hilt, Christine B. Cha, and Susan Nolen-Hoeksema, "Nonsuicidal self-injury in young adolescent girls: Moderators of the distress-function relationship," *Journal of Consulting and Clinical Psychology* 76, no. 1 (February 2008): 63–71.

CHAPTER 6: GROWING UP

1. A. H. Maslow, "A Theory of Metamotivation," *Journal of Humanistic Psychology* 7, no. 2 (1967): 93–127; A. H. Maslow, "The Farther Reaches of Human Nature," *Journal of Transpersonal Psychology* 1, no. 1 (1969): 1–9.

CHAPTER 8: AN OVERZEALOUS ASSISTANT

1. Eric Thomas, "Half of SoCal Sea Lion Pups Have Died This Winter," *Malibu Times*, March 30, 2013, www.malibutimes .com/news/article_48007dce-9970-11e2-ad51-001a4bcf887a .html.
2. Merriam-Webster Online, s.v. "ego," www.merriam-webster .com/dictionary/ego.
3. Ibid.

CHAPTER TEN: UNITY DISGUISED

1. Candace B. Pert, PhD, *Molecules of Emotion* (New York: Touchstone, 1997).

CHAPTER 11: THE EGO MAKES ITS ENTRANCE

1. Cate Montana, *Unearthing Venus: My Search for the Woman Within* (London: Watkins, 2013).

CHAPTER 12: BODIES "R" US

1. Joe Dispenza, *Breaking the Habit of Being Yourself* (Carlsbad, CA: Hay House, 2013).

CHAPTER 13: HOW THE EGO IS BORN

1. George Markowsky, "Information Theory, Mathematics," *Encyclopedia Britannica Online*, www.britannica.com/topic /information-theory.

2. Ibid.

3. Patricia L. Davies, Wen-Pin Chang, and William L. Gavin, "Maturation of Sensory Gating Performance in Children with and without Sensory Processing Disorders," *International Journal of Psychophysiology* 72, no. 2 (May 2009): 187–97.

4. Cold Spring Harbor Laboratory, "Researchers Uncover Scaffolds in the Brain's Wiring Diagram," *ScienceDaily*, March 13, 2005, www.sciencedaily.com/releases/2004/07/04072309 3056.htm.

5. Martin Hilbert and Pricila López, "The World's Technological Capacity to Store, Communicate, and Compute Information," *Science* 332, no. 6025 (April 2011): 60–65.

6. M. Lewis and J. Brooks-Gunn, *Social Cognition and the Acquisition of Self* (New York: Plenum Press, 1979).

CHAPTER 15: THE NATURE OF REALITY

1. Milo Wolff and Geoff Haselhurst, "Light and the Electron, Einstein's Last Question," presented at Beyond Einstein, Stanford University, May 2004.

2. Lynne McTaggart, *The Intention Experiment* (New York: HarperElement, 2007).

3. Stuart Hameroff and Deepak Chopra, "The Quantum Soul Part 2: The Quantum World and Fine Scale of the Universe," Deepak Chopra newsletter, January 21, 2012, www.deepak chopra.com/blog/article/3500.

4. Cate Montana, personal notes from interview with Dr. Stuart Hameroff, 2006.

5. David Bohm, *Wholeness and the Implicate Order* (New York: Routledge, 2002).

6. Erwin Schrödinger, *What Is Life? With Mind and Matter*

and Autobiographical Sketches (London: Cambridge University Press, 2012).

7. Swami Muktananda, *I Am That*, fourth ed. (New York: Siddha Yoga Publications, 1992).

CHAPTER 16: THE LIVING UNIVERSE

1. M. Tegmark and A. Vilenkin, "The Case for Parallel Universes," *Scientific American*, July 19, 2011; G. Ellis, "Does the Multiverse Really Exist?" *Scientific American*, August 1, 2011; Joshua Sokol, "Mystery Bright Spots Could Be First Glimpse of Another Universe," *New Scientist*, October 28, 2015.

2. E. Siegal, "How Many Galaxies Are There in the Universe? The Redder We Look, the More We See," *Discover*, October 10, 2012.

3. S. Borenstein, "8.8 billion habitable Earth-size planets exist in Milky Way alone," quoted on *NBC Nightly News*, NBC, November 4, 2013.

4. University of Wisconsin–Madison, "Physicists Find Way to 'See' Extra Dimensions," *Science Daily*, February 4, 2007, www.sciencedaily.com/releases/2007/02/070203103355.htm.

5. Duane Elgin, *The Living Universe* (San Francisco: Berrett-Koehler Publishers, 2009).

6. John G. Neihardt, *Black Elk Speaks* (Lincoln, NE: Bison Books, 2014).

7. M. Gagliano, et al., "Toward Understanding Plant Bioacoustics," *Trends in Plant Science* 17, no. 6 (2012): 323–25.

8. Dan Cossins, "Plant Talk," *The Scientist*, January 1, 2014.

9. Ibid.

10. David Storoy, "David Bohm, Implicate Order and

Holomovement," *Science & Nonduality*, scienceandnon
duality.com/david-bohm-implicate-order-and
-holomovement.

11. Duane Elgin, *The Living Universe* (San Francisco: Berrett-
Koehler Publishers, 2009).

12. Ibid.

13. Gretchen Reynolds, "How Walking in Nature Changes
the Brain," *New York Times*, July 22, 2015, well.blogs
.nytimes.com/2015/07/22/how-nature-changes-the-brain
/?_r=0.

CHAPTER 17: PERCEPTION IS . . . EVERYTHING

1. "Thou madest him a little lower than the angels; thou
crownedst him with glory and honour, and didst set him
over the works of thy hands": Hebrews 2:7 (KJV).

2. Rosies Tanabe, "Rubin Vase," *New World Encyclopedia*,
July 20, 2015, www.newworldencyclopedia.org/p/index.php
?title=Rubin_vase&oldid=989525.

3. Ken Wilber, "Supermind and the Primordial Avoidance,"
Integral Life, January 18, 2015, www.integrallife.com/loft
-series/supermind-and-primordial-avoidance.

CHAPTER 18: GETTING IT TOGETHER

1. Candace B. Pert, PhD, *Molecules of Emotion* (New York:
Touchstone, 1997).

CHAPTER 20: THE THREE MINDS

1. Lifestyles of Health and Sustainability, www.LOHAS.com.

CHAPTER 22: EXTRA BAGGAGE

1. Matthew 7:13–14 (KJV).

CHAPTER 23: THE LAW OF ATTRACTION

1. HeartMath Institute, "The Energetic Heart Is Unfolding," July 22, 2010, www.heartmath.org/articles-of-the-heart /science-of-the-heart/the-energetic-heart-is-unfolding.
2. Ibid.

CHAPTER 25: THE IMITATION GAME

1. Agostino Bono, "John Jay Study Reveals Extent of Abuse Problem," Catholic News Service, www.americancatholic .org/news/clergysexabuse/johnjaycns.asp.
2. Deborah Caldwell, "Vatican Finances: CNBC Explains," CNBC, March 14, 2013, www.cnbc.com/id/100554748.

CHAPTER 26: THE REAL DEAL

1. Francis E. Kuo and Andrea F. Taylor, "A Potential Natural Treatment for Attention-Deficit/Hyperactivity Disorder: Evidence from a National Study," *American Journal of Public Health* 94, no. 9 (September 2004): 1580–86.

SUGGESTED READING

Chasse, Betsy. *Tipping Sacred Cows*. New York: Atria, Beyond Words, 2014.

Dispenza, Joe. *Breaking the Habit of Being Yourself: How to Lose Your Mind and Create a New One*. Carlsbad, CA: Hay House, 2013.

———. *Evolve Your Brain: The Science of Changing Your Mind*. Deerfield Beach, FL: Health Communications, 2008.

Elgin, Duane. *The Living Universe*. San Francisco: Berrett-Koehler Publishers, 2009.

———. *Voluntary Simplicity*. New York: Harper, 2010.

Foundation for Inner Peace. *A Course in Miracles*. Mill Valley, CA: 2008.

Goswami, Amit. *The Self-Aware Universe: How Consciousness Creates the Material World*. New York: Tarcher, 1995.

Greene, Brian. *The Elegant Universe: Superstrings, Hidden Dimensions, and the Quest for the Ultimate Theory*. New York: W. W. Norton and Co., 2010.

Hawking, Stephen. *The Theory of Everything*. Mumbai: Jaico Publishing House, 2007.

Hill, Napoleon. *Outwitting the Devil: The Secret to Freedom and Success*. New York: Sterling, 2012.

Lind, Richard, PhD. *The Seeking Self: The Quest for Self-Improvement & the Creation of Personal Suffering*. Grand Rapids, MI: Phanes Press, 2000.

Lipton, Bruce. *The Biology of Belief: Unleashing the Power of Consciousness, Matter & Miracles*. Carlsbad, CA: Hay House, 2007.

Maslow, Abraham H. *The Farther Reaches of Human Nature*. New York: Penguin/Arkana, 1993.

———. *Toward a Psychology of Being*. Hoboken, NJ: Sublime Books, 2014.

McKenna, Jed. *Jed McKenna's Theory of Everything: The Enlightened Perspective*. San Francisco: Wisefool Press, 2013.

———. *Spiritual Enlightenment: The Damnedest Thing*. San Francisco: Wisefool Press, 2011.

McTaggart, Lynne. *The Field*. New York: HarperPerennial 2008.

———. *The Intention Experiment*. New York: HarperElement, 2007.

Penrose, Sir Roger. *Shadows of the Mind: A Search for the Missing Science of Consciousness*. New York: Oxford University Press, 1994.

———. *The Road to Reality: A Complete Guide to the Laws of the Universe*. New York: Vintage Books, 2007.

Renard, Gary. *Disappearance of the Universe*, revised edition. Carlsbad, CA: Hay House, 2004.

———. *Your Immortal Reality: How to Break the Cycle of Birth and Death*. Carlsbad, CA: Hay House, 2007.

Rosenblum, Bruce, and Fred Kuttner. *Quantum Enigma*. New York: Oxford University Press, 2011.

Rudd, Richard. *The Gene Keys: Unlocking the Higher Purpose Hidden in Your DNA*. London: Watkins Publishing, 2013.

Talbot, Michael. *The Holographic Universe*. New York: HarperPerennial, 2011.

Tolle, Eckhart. *Stillness Speaks*. New York: New World Library, 2003.

———. *The Power of Now*. Vancouver: Namaste Publishing, 2004.

Vasudev, Sadhguru Jaggi. *Encounter the Enlightened: Conversations with the Master*. New Delhi: Isha Yoga Foundation, 2001.

———. *Inner Engineering: A Yogi's Guide to Joy*. New York: Spiegel & Grau, 2016.

———. *Mystic Musings*. New Delhi: Isha Yoga Foundation, 2003.

Wilber, Ken. *A Brief History of Everything*. Boston: Shambhala, 2001.

———. *Integral Spirituality: A Startling New Role for Religion in the Modern and Postmodern World*. Boston: Integral Books, 2006.

MOVIES

Cosmos: A Spacetime Odyssey (series with Neil deGrasse Tyson)

Groundhog Day, 1993 (best movie ever on the evolution of the ego through the needs hierarchy. And *funny!*)

Kung Fu Panda 1 (2008) and *Kung Fu Panda 3* (2016)

MindWalk, 1990

One: The Movie, 2005

Particle Fever, 2013

The Matrix, 1999

What the Bleep Do We Know!?, 2004

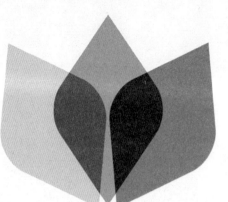

ENLIVEN™

About Our Books: We are the world's first holistic publisher for mission-driven authors. We curate, create, collaborate on, and commission sophisticated, fresh titles and voices to enhance your spiritual development, success, and wellness pursuits.

About Our Vision: Our authors are the voice of empowerment, creativity, and spirituality in the twenty-first century. You, our readers, are brilliant seekers of adventure, unexpected stories, and tools to transform yourselves and your world. Together, we are change-makers on a mission to increase literacy, uplift humanity, ignite genius, and create reasons to gather around books. We think of ourselves as instigators of soulful exchange.

Enliven Books is a new imprint from social entrepreneur and publisher Zhena Muzyka, author of *Life by the Cup*.

To explore our list of books and learn about fresh new voices in the realm of Mind-Body-Spirit, please visit us at

EnlivenBooks.com | **f/EnlivenBooks**